Reading English News
On the Internet

A Guide to

Connectors

Verbs

Expressions &

Vocabulary

For the ESL Student

Plus tips and strategies to help make sense of

online NEWS, BUSINESS and SPORTS articles

Dr. David Petersen

Reading English News on the Internet (General Edition)
A Guide to Connectors, Verbs, Expressions, and Vocabulary for the ESL
Student

Clipart used under Terms of Use at WPClipart
(http://www.wpclipart.com/legal.html)

Crosswords used with kind permission of EclipseCrossword
http://www.eclipsecrossword.com

Published by Lulu Press, Morrisville, NC, USA

ISBN 978-1-84753-977-9

Feedback to reading.english.news@gmail.com

Dedicated to SuperMandy

For the Teacher

The purpose of this book is to help ESL learners at the intermediate level with the potentially confusing turns of phrase common to English articles online, in magazines and in newspapers. ESL veterans will appreciate that while many books cover English grammar and vocabulary, there are precious few dealing specifically with idioms, "quirky" verbs, and other compound constructs from a practical perspective. My goal has been to create a workbook systematic enough to integrate easily into a variety of academic contexts, making the learning experience as efficient and painless as possible.

This book actually stems from my experiences as a Japanese translator. Working at an agency in Hiroshima, I was struck by the number of questions I was fielding from coworkers trying to make sense of English newspaper articles and other challenging documents. On closer inspection, most of the difficulties seemed to involve idioms ("on the loose", "public outcry"), constructs that are poorly covered in many textbooks and are difficult to look up due to their compound nature. In discussing this issue with friends and teachers it became apparent that related grammar elements such as connectors ("as...as a...") and verbs of one type or another ("to show promise") present similar problems for non-native speakers. I began collecting examples of the most commonly misunderstood "offenders", and ultimately put together the manuscript over the course of about two years.

Applications: On one level, the book functions as a simple guide to the meanings of nearly 200 connectors, phrasal verbs, idiomatic verb-phrases, and expressions. Individual sections can also be introduced a few pages at a time into almost any classroom situation, gradually building English comprehension. To develop full lessons of 40 minutes or more, I would recommend supplementation with materials on mass-media, the internet, and current events. The "tips" sections on website content deal with the typical structure of online articles, and are best covered as part of a writing class with internet access. The mini-quizzes at the end of each unit provide immediate feedback about the progress of the students, and can also serve as a template for the creation of your own tests and exams

Lesson Overview

The vocabulary in this book is divided into three major sections:

- Connectors ("provided that", "in spite of") linking two or more phrases or sentences together
- Verbs with an emphasis on phrasal verbs ("to pull out of", "to put into") and idiomatic verb phrases ("to burn the midnight oil")
- Expressions ("a meeting of the minds", "a matter of time")

Each entry is organized as follows:

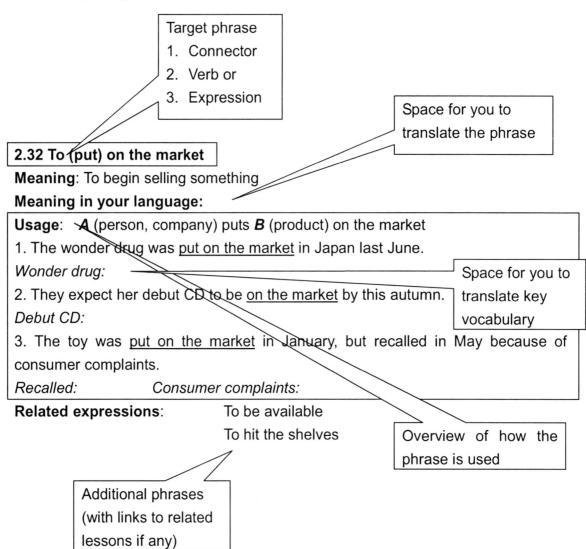

Target phrase
1. Connector
2. Verb or
3. Expression

Space for you to translate the phrase

2.32 To (put) on the market

Meaning: To begin selling something

Meaning in your language:

Usage: A (person, company) puts **B** (product) on the market

1. The wonder drug was <u>put on the market</u> in Japan last June.

Wonder drug:

2. They expect her debut CD to be <u>on the market</u> by this autumn.

Debut CD:

3. The toy was <u>put on the market</u> in January, but recalled in May because of consumer complaints.

Recalled: *Consumer complaints:*

Space for you to translate key vocabulary

Related expressions: To be available

                                 To hit the shelves

Overview of how the phrase is used

Additional phrases (with links to related lessons if any)

The Tips Sections

These mini-lessons deal with the nitty gritty of finding articles online, navigating a typical website, understanding differences in vocabulary and style by topic, and anticipating structure so as to increase reading efficiency. Each section can stand alone, but is also suitable for development as a classroom exercise, particularly if internet access is available.

TIPS I: A list of basic computer-related vocabulary

TIPS II: A list of popular English-language news websites

TIPS III: Typical vocabulary required for registration and for logging in to websites.

TIPS IV: Guide to online news articles, covering structure, vocabulary, and
            reading strategies

TIPS V: A list of useful business and financial websites

TIPS VI: Getting the most out of business and financial articles

TIPS VII: A list of popular sporting news websites

TIPS VIII: Features of online sporting news

A world of English awaits….

TABLE OF CONTENTS

Section I: Connectors

1.1 As a

Meaning: Talking about someone's role, title, or rank

Meaning in your language:

Usage: As an *A* (role, title, rank)

1. He has been working <u>as a</u> medical x-ray technician since he graduated from vocational college.

Medical x-ray technician: *Vocational college:*

2. He first came to Japan <u>as a</u> tourist, but later returned as a United Nations goodwill ambassador.

Tourist: *United Nations:*

Goodwill ambassador:

3. The medical establishment has strong doubts that the herb is useful <u>as a</u> cancer treatment.

Medical establishment: *To have doubts:*

Herbs: *Cancer treatment:*

Related expressions: Moonlighting as

Making a living as

She works as an astronaut

1.2 As far as... is concerned

Meaning: Explaining someone's viewpoint or opinion

Meaning in your language:

Usage: As far as *A* (person) is concerned *B* (viewpoint, opinion)

1. <u>As far as</u> I <u>am concerned</u>, you don't have to finish the work today, but the boss may disagree.

To finish the work today:

2. <u>As far as</u> the credit agency <u>is concerned</u>, the most important thing in the world is financial security.

Credit agency:

The most important thing in the world:

Financial security:

3. <u>As far as</u> our company <u>is concerned</u>, the sales this year were very disappointing.

The sales this year:

Related expressions: From where I'm sitting

The way I see it

As far as I'm concerned, education is very important

19

1.3 As opposed to

Meaning: Comparison of two things that are very different

Meaning in your language:

Usage: *A* (situation), as opposed to *B* (opposite situation)

1. I did very well in academic endeavors, <u>as opposed to</u> my brother, who excelled at basketball and other sports.

Academic endeavors: *Excel at sports:*

2. Metropolitan Tokyo is a crowded place to live, <u>as opposed to</u> Hokkaido, which has very few people.

Crowded: *Metropolitan Tokyo:*

3. Australia collected 16 medals at the Olympics, <u>as opposed to</u> Canada, which collected only 1.

To collect a medal:

Related expressions: Like night and day

                                    Worlds apart

1.4 Be that as it may

Meaning: Something is true, but that doesn't change the situation.

Meaning in your language:

Usage: *A* (fact). Be that as it may, *B* (fact, action)

1. I have a bad cold. <u>Be that as it may</u>, I still have to go to work today.

Bad cold: *Go to work:*

2. It's true that I don't love your sister. <u>Be that as it may</u>, I promised her that I would marry her, so I have no choice.

To promise to marry:

3. Yes, I know I'm in the kitchen. <u>Be that as it may</u>, I've got my hands full at the moment - make your own cup of tea!

Got my hands full: *To make tea:*

Related expressions: Even though

                                    In any case

1.5 Considering (the / that / how)

Meaning: Something is true, but only because of the situation.

Meaning in your language:

Usage: *A* (fact, opinion), considering that *B* (qualified, point of view)

1. The weather is very hot today, <u>considering the</u> time of year.

Time of year:

2. He did very well on his bar exam, <u>considering that</u> he cut classes and didn't study all year.

To do well on a test: *Bar exam:*

Cut classes:

3. The new DVD player sold quite well, <u>considering how</u> little advertising it had in the newspapers and on television.

To sell well: *Advertising:*

Related expressions: All things considered

Given that…

1.6 Even so

Meaning: "I agree with you, but I am not changing my mind."

Meaning in your language:

Usage: *A* (fact). Even so, *B* (contrary fact)

1. I agree that the movie was overly long. <u>Even so</u>, the acting was great and I really enjoyed it.

Overly long: *Acting is great:*

2. Yes, I agree that he is a rather dull person. <u>Even so</u>, he's the best accountant our company has ever employed.

Dull person: *Accountant:*

3. Yes, I know that it may rain later. <u>Even so</u>, I'm going on the picnic.

Picnic:

Related expressions: Nonetheless

Be that as it may

1.7 If worse comes to worst

Meaning: Imagining a bad outcome; being pessimistic

Meaning in your language:

Usage: If worse comes to worst, *A* (action, plan)

1. <u>If worse comes to worst</u> and I'm still sick tomorrow morning, then I will stay in bed.

To stay in bed (when sick):

2. <u>If worse comes to worst</u> and I can't get tomorrow off, I will telephone you.

To get tomorrow off:

3. <u>If worse comes to worst</u> and he is forced to resign from politics, at least he can find work as a public speaker.

To resign from politics: *Public speaker:*

Related expressions: Worst-case scenario

If it comes to that

If worse comes to worst, we can always finish tomorrow

1.8 (In a) bid to / for

Meaning: Someone is trying to get something.

Meaning in your language:

Usage:　In a bid to **A** (goal), **B** (person, group) does **C** (action)

1. The new tax cuts are part of the mayor's <u>bid for</u> re-election.

A tax cut:　　　　　*Mayor:*　　　　　*Re-election:*

2. <u>In a bid to</u> stop the protestors, the company offered to move the new construction site away from the riverbank.

Protestors:　　　　　　*Construction site:*

Building site:

3. <u>In a bid to</u> improve the city image, City Hall decided that all municipal buses would be repainted.

City Hall:　　　　*Municipal buses:*　　　　*To repaint:*

Related expressions:　　　　In an attempt to

In the hope that

1.9 In anticipation of

Meaning: Preparation for an event

Meaning in your language:

Usage:　In anticipation of **A** (prediction), **B** (person, group) does **C** (action)

1. The logging company started a promotional campaign <u>in anticipation of</u> resistance from local residents and environmental groups.

Logging company:　　　　*Promotional campaign:*

Environmental groups:

2. <u>In anticipation of</u> a big lawsuit, the chemical factory offered the widow a large sum of money.

Lawsuit:　　　　*Chemical factory:*　　　　*Widow:*

3. The boutique hired new staff <u>in anticipation of</u> the Christmas rush.

Boutique:　　　*To hire:*　　　*Christmas rush:*

Related expressions:　　　　Looking ahead

With an eye to

1.10 In response to

Meaning: As one thing changes, so does another thing.

Meaning in your language:

Usage: In response to *A* (event, circumstances), *B* (action)

1. <u>In response to</u> strong public pressure, the planning department has decided to cancel the construction of the new airport.

Public pressure: *Planning department:*

Construction:

2. <u>In response to</u> the increasing spread of HIV, the government is starting a new education program for teenagers.

The spread of HIV: *Education program:*

3. The concert has been moved to next weekend <u>in response to</u> the flooding of the arena.

Moved to next week: *Flooding:*   *Arena:*

Related expressions: In accordance with

          Based on

 Famous Saying

No act of kindness, no matter how small, is ever wasted. (See 1.15)
(Aesop 620 to 560 BC)

1.11 In spite of

Meaning: Action is taken, even though the situation is dangerous or difficult.

Meaning in your language:

Usage: In spite of **A** (circumstances), **B** (action)
1. <u>In spite of</u> the incredible heat wave, many people came to the festival.
Incredible: *Heat wave:*
2. He said that he will remain a sports commentator <u>in spite of</u> the growing scandal.
Sports commentator: *Growing scandal:*
3. The car company was confident that it would succeed, <u>in spite of</u> the recent poor sales performance.
Car company: *To succeed:*
Sales performance:

Related expressions: Despite

Against all odds

It was a good picnic, in spite of the ants

1.12 Instead of

Meaning #1: Describing alternatives

Meaning in your language:

Usage: Instead of **A** (action), **B** (another action)
1. <u>Instead of</u> quarreling all the time, why don't you try to listen to each other?
Quarreling:
2. <u>Instead of</u> eating at home last night, we went out to a fancy restaurant.
Fancy restaurant:
Meaning #2: The result was unexpected; the opposite thing happened.
Meaning in your language:
1. <u>Instead of</u> helping his fever, the medicine only made his condition worse.
Fever: *Condition:*
2. To everyone's surprise, <u>instead of</u> approving the new legislation, the governor vetoed the bill.
To approve legislation: *Governor:*
To veto a bill:

Related expressions: Rather than (Meaning #1)

Out of the blue (Meaning #2)

 Famous Saying

What lies behind us and what lies ahead of us are tiny matters, compared to what lives within us. (See 2.47)

(Henry David Thoreau 1817-1862)

1.13 In the event of

Meaning: If one thing happens, something else will too.

Meaning in your language:

Usage: In the event of *A* (situation), *B* (action)

1. <u>In the event of</u> a fire, please use the stairs, not the elevator.

Fire: *Elevator:*

2. Train services will be stopped temporarily <u>in the event of</u> an earthquake.

Stopped temporarily: *Earthquake:*

3. <u>In the event of</u> a bus strike, many people will have to find other ways of
   getting to work.

A strike:

Related expressions: In case of

In an emergency

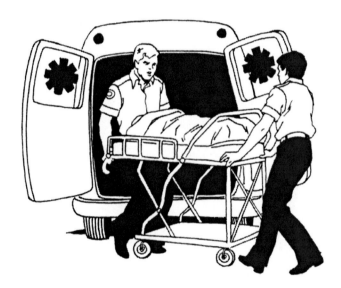

In the event of an emergency, call the paramedics

1.14 In the wake of

Meaning: A recent event is still having an effect (usually a bad effect).

Meaning in your language:

Usage: In the wake of **A** (event), **B** (action, effect)

1. <u>In the wake of</u> the recent terrorist incidents, airport security has really been tightened.

Terrorist incidents: *Tightening of security:*

2. Everyone was evacuated from the building <u>in the wake of</u> the bomb threat.

To evacuate a building: *Bomb threat:*

3. Many jobs were lost <u>in the wake of</u> the economic downturn.

Economic downturn:

Related expressions: In the aftermath of

          To have no alternative but to (See 2.43)

1.15 No matter how much / far / hard

Meaning: Something remains the same, despite something else.

Meaning in your language:

Usage: No matter how much **A** (person, organization) **B** (action), **C** (unchanging situation)

1. <u>No matter how hard</u> I try, I just can't get her to agree with me.

To agree with:

2. <u>No matter how much</u> I exercise, I just can't seem to lose weight.

Exercise: *To lose weight:*

3. <u>No matter how far</u> he travels, he always comes home for the holidays.

Home for the holidays:

Related expressions: Try as I might

          Wasted effort

1.16 Not only... but also

Meaning: Giving extra information about something

Meaning in your language:

Usage: ...not only **A** (person, group) but also **B** (person, group)

1. The recent fare increase is upsetting <u>not only</u> everyday commuters <u>but also</u> the tourists as well.

Fare increase: *To upset:*   *Commuters:*

2. The severe tropical storm is going to disrupt <u>not only</u> train service <u>but also</u> the delivery of mail.

Tropical storm: *To disrupt:*

Delivery:

3. The change in scholarship regulations affects <u>not only</u> new students <u>but also</u> previously enrolled students.

Scholarship regulations: *Previously enrolled:*

Related expressions: In addition to

                                    What's more

 **Famous Saying**

It's hard to make a comeback when you haven't been anywhere.
(see 2.48)
(Anonymous)

1.17 On account of

Meaning: Because of; as a result of

Meaning in your language:

Usage: On account of **A** (cause), **B** (effect)

1. The outdoor jazz concert in the park last weekend was cancelled <u>on account of</u> the rain.

   Jazz: *Outdoor concert:*

2. My head office was forced to close <u>on account of</u> the terrible economic conditions last year.

   Forced to close: *Economic conditions:*

3. <u>On account of</u> the traffic accident, Highway No.1 was blocked off by the police for several hours.

   Traffic accident: *Blocked off:*

Related expressions: Owing to

                              Due to

The trip was cancelled on account of the rain

1.18 On the other hand

Meaning: Looking at something in a different way; seeing another side of a problem

Meaning in your language:

Usage: *A* (fact, situation). On the other hand, *B* (fact, situation)

1. The weather this summer has been too rainy for me. <u>On the other hand</u>, it's been good for the farmers.

Too rainy: *Farmers:*

2. He should resign because he's a corrupt politician. <u>On the other hand</u>, most politicians are corrupt...

To resign: *Corrupt politician:*

3. The lecture was far too long. <u>On the other hand</u>, the speaker did raise a lot of interesting points.

Lecture: *Speaker:*   *To raise a point:*

Related expressions: The other side of the coin

The flip side

1.19 Provided (that)

Meaning: Something will happen later, but only if something else happens first.

Meaning in your language:

Usage: *A* (plan for the future) provided *B* (conditions)

1. I'm going to study abroad next year, <u>provided</u> I can raise enough money for the trip.

To study abroad: *To raise money:*

2. The music store plans to open a new branch in our city, <u>provided that</u> they can find a suitable building lot.

Suitable: *Building lot:*

3. The governor will be released from the hospital tomorrow afternoon, <u>provided that</u> his condition is stable.

Released from hospital: *Condition is stable:*

Related expressions: (Just as) as long as

Fingers crossed

1.20 Speaking of

Meaning: One topic reminds someone of another topic, and the conversation changes.

Meaning in your language:

Usage: Speaking of *A* (topic), *B* (related topic)

1. <u>Speaking of</u> Beckham's change of venue, do you think it'll benefit MLS?

Change of venue: *MLS: Major League Soccer (US)*

2. <u>Speaking of</u> new places to eat, I really enjoyed lunch at that new Italian restaurant uptown.

Italian restaurant: *Uptown:*

3. <u>Speaking of</u> government spending, I think the new road works project is totally unnecessary.

Government spending: *Road works project:*

Unnecessary:

Related expressions: Now that you mention it

Come to think of it

Speaking of money… how's your new part-time job?

1.21 Thanks to

Meaning: Some action had a good effect.

Meaning in your language:

Usage: Thanks to *A* (cause), *B* (effect)

1. Thanks to the recent revolution in technology, it is now possible to watch movies over the internet.

Revolution in technology:

2. Thanks to his kind reference letter, I was able to find a good job.

Reference letter:

3. I am approaching success now as an artist, thanks to your steadfast confidence in me.

Approach success: *Steadfast:*

Related expressions: Because of

To credit…to (See 2.17)

1.22 That / Which is to say

Meaning: Summarizing a situation, or recommending action

Meaning in your language:

Usage: *A* (facts). That is to say *B* (summary of the same facts)

1. Annual temperatures are rising and the polar ice caps are melting. That is to say, global warming is a serious problem.

Annual temperatures: *Polar ice caps:*

Global warming:

2. He lost his last job because he's a drinker, and he hasn't worked in two years. That is to say, we shouldn't hire him.

To lose a job: *A drinker:*

3. She is appearing in a new Steelberg movie, and she just won an Oscar. Which is to say, she's the hottest star in Hollywood.

Appearing in a new … movie:

To win an Oscar:

Related expressions: In other words

To make a long story short (See 1.26)

1.23 Through

Meaning: An outcome is the result of something else.

Meaning in your language:

Usage: Through *A* (cause), *B* (result)

1. The homeless center is only kept open <u>through</u> gifts from concerned parties.

Homeless center: *Kept open:*

Concerned parties:

2. His physical fitness goals can only be reached <u>through</u> strong commitment.

Physical fitness: *To reach:*   *Commitment:*

3. It seems that the dispute between the two groups may only be settled <u>through</u> litigation.

To settle: *A dispute:*   *Litigation:*

Related expressions: Thanks to (See 1.21)

                                    By

1.24 To a certain extent... (but)

Meaning: Something is partly true, but something else is also true.

Meaning in your language:

Usage: To a certain extent *A* (fact), but *B* (another fact)

1. <u>To a certain extent</u>, the party was a waste of time, <u>but</u> at least I got to see some old friends again.

Waste of time: *Old friends:*

2. The candidate said that <u>to a certain extent</u>, she is glad that she lost the election, because it gives her more time to be with her family.

Candidate: *To lose the election:*

3. <u>To a certain extent</u>, it's sad that city is tearing down the old buildings, <u>but</u> it's also a chance to improve the neighborhood.

Tearing down: *Neighborhood:*

Related expressions: As far as it goes

                                    True enough, (but)

1.25 To be on the safe side

Meaning: Being extremely careful

Meaning in your language:

Usage: To be on the safe side, **A** (person, group) **B** (action)

1. Even though the tests were negative, the doctor decided to remove the lump to be on the safe side.

Negative test results: *To remove a lump:*

2. You should bring two flashlights when you climb Mt. Fuji, to be on the safe side.

Flashlights:

3. Bring an umbrella with you just to be on the safe side. It might rain later.

Umbrella:

Related expressions: To play it safe

To hedge one's bets

1.26 To make a long story short

Meaning: Summarizing something, or restating it

Meaning in your language:

Usage: **A** (facts). To make a long story short **B** (summary of the same facts)

1. I lost my wallet and forgot my car keys, and then missed the bus. To make a long story short, it's been a bad day.

To lose one's wallet: *To miss the bus:*

2. He's a hit with the teenage set, and he's on television all the time. To make a long story short, he's a superstar.

A hit with: *Superstar:*

3. The Minister for Finance is meeting with the bank managers now, and then he's flying to Tokyo for a press conference. To make a long story short, his schedule is completely full today.

Minister for Finance: *Press conference:*

Schedule is full:

Related expressions: The gist of the matter

That is to say (See 1.22)

35

1.27 Whatever it takes

Meaning: Someone plans to do something, even if it is difficult or expensive.

Meaning in your language:

Usage: *A* (person, group) does whatever it takes to *B* (achieve some goal)
1. Since I've enrolled in graduate school, I'll do <u>whatever it takes</u> to get my degree.
To enroll: *To get a degree:*
2. The explorers say that they will do <u>whatever it takes</u> to reach the top of Mt. Everest.
To reach the top:
3. She'll do <u>whatever it takes</u> to get that promotion, even if it means working overtime every night.
To get a promotion: *To work overtime:*

Related expressions: Dead set on

Do or die

1.28 What's more

Meaning: Making an extra point; adding more information

Meaning in your language:

Usage: *A* (fact). What's more, *B* (another fact)
1. That restaurant was terrible. The service was bad, and <u>what's more</u>, the prices were high.
Bad service at a restaurant:
2. The temperature was very hot yesterday. <u>What's more</u>, it was very humid.
Humid:
3. She's a very good business woman. She's clever and <u>what's more,</u> she's got good people skills.
Business woman: *Clever:*   *People skills:*

Related expressions: If that weren't enough

Moreover

Mini-Quiz: Connectors

Part A

1.Her first job was working …. waiter during the summer.
a) provided that   **b)** as a   **c)** in the event of   **d)** that is to say

2.You shouldn't marry him – he's unkind and ... he's very unreliable.
a) if worse comes to worst   **b)** be that as it may   **c)** thanks to   **d)** what's more

3.If you continue to study …good times and bad, you will get your degree.
a) Speaking of   **b)** Considering that   **c)** through   **d)** In a bid to

4.My boyfriend is from a poor family. … I intend to marry him.
a) Be that as it may   **b)** As opposed to   **c)** On account of   **d)** On the other hand

5.He graduated from university … his learning disabilities.
a) as a   **b)** what's more   **c)** thanks to   **d)** in spite of

6.The department store is giving away free beer … attract customers.
a) in a bid to   **b)** in the wake of   **c)** be that as it may   **d)** even so

7.She said that …it costs, she is going find a cure for her son's illness.
a) in a move to   **b)** even so   **c)** no matter how much   **d)** to a certain extent

8.… is vitamin C good for general health … it may also help to prevent colds.

a) As far as … is concerned   **b**) To a certain extent … but   **c)** Over time

d) Not only…but

9. Mark is good at baseball,… David, who is good at good at soccer.

a) on account of   **b)** as opposed to   **c)** even so   **d)** thanks to

10. It might rain, so … you should bring an umbrella.

a) to be on the safe side   **b)** if worse comes to worse   **c)** in the event of

d) provided that

11.…changing jobs is concerned, wait until you have more savings in the bank.

a) Considering that   **b)** As far as **c)** In anticipation of   **d)** On the other hand

12. Your health is in danger. Do … to stay well.

a) instead of   **b)** provided that   **c)** if worse comes to worse **d)** whatever it takes

13. DEF brand soap costs less than most. … our quality is unsurpassed.

a) Even so,   **b)** As a   **c)** through   **d)** Speaking of

14. This building method may prove invaluable … an earthquake.

a) in spite of   **b)** in the event of   **c)** instead of   **d)** through

15. Winds are still strong … last night's typhoon.

a) as opposed to   **b)** in response to   **c)** in the wake of   **d)** on the other hand

Part B

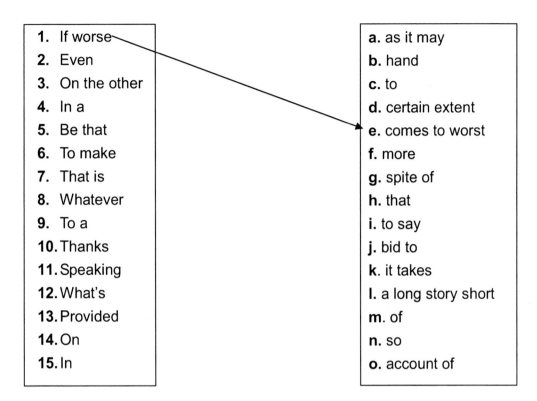

1. If worse	a. as it may
2. Even	b. hand
3. On the other	c. to
4. In a	d. certain extent
5. Be that	e. comes to worst
6. To make	f. more
7. That is	g. spite of
8. Whatever	h. that
9. To a	i. to say
10. Thanks	j. bid to
11. Speaking	k. it takes
12. What's	l. a long story short
13. Provided	m. of
14. On	n. so
15. In	o. account of

Part C

E.g. may / that / as / be / it : <u>Be that as it may</u>

1. worse / worst / to / if / comes   : _____
2. event / in / of / the   : _____
3. in / of / the / wake   : _____
4. no / much / matter / how   : _____
5. on / other / the / hand   : _____
6. is / to / say / that   : _____
7. certain / a / to / extent   : _____
8. safe / side / to / on / be / the   : _____
9. long / short / story / to / make / a   : _____
10. is / far / as / … / concerned / as   : _____

I'm going to learn English, whatever it takes (see 1.27)

TIPS I: Basic Computer-Related Vocabulary

Here are some common words and phrases related to computers and the internet.

Hardware-Related Terms

English	Your Language	
CD (compact disk) drive		
Computer chip		
CPU / central processing unit		
CRT / cathode ray tube		
Desktop computer		
DVD (digital versatile disk) drive		
Flash memory		
Flat screen		
Hard drive		
Keyboard		
Laptop computer		
Memory slot		

41

Hardware Continued

English	Your Language	
Motherboard		
Mouse		
PC / personal computer		
Peripherals		
Power supply		
RAM / random access Memory		
ROM / read-only memory		
Router		
USB (universal serial bus) hub, port		
Webcam		

Computer (Internet) Operations

English	Your Language	
Click (on a link)		
Close (a tab, an app)		
Copy (text, a file)		
Download (a file)		
Google (a term)		
Log in (to a website)		
Log out (of a website)		
Open (a file, a webpage)		
Paste (text, a file)		
Reboot		
Reload (a page)		
Restart		
Right-click (on a link)		
Save / save as		
Search for (a file, a term)		
Shutdown		
Startup		
Surf (the net)		

Other Computer-Related Terms

English	Your Language	
ADSL (Asymmetric Digital Subscriber Line) connection		
App / application		
Avatar		
Blog / web-log		
Broadband connection		
Email access		
Facebook profile		
Form / registration form		
Home network		
Internet access		
Instant messaging		
LAN (local area network) connection		
Menu / dropdown menu		
Online (news, shopping)		
OS / operating system		
P2P / peer-to-peer		
Password		
RSS (Really Simple Syndication) feed		
Search engine		
Social networking (site)		
Software		
Streaming (audio, video)		
Twitter / micro-blogging		
URL / computer address		
Username		
Web (2.0, access, address, browser, page, site)		

Tips I – Crossword

Across

2. Reload a ___
4. ___ computer
5. ___ shopping
6. Download ___
10. ___ access
11. Search ___
12. ___ ray tube
13. Surf the ___

Down

1. Home ___
2. Central ___ unit
3. Click on a ___
7. Flat ____
8. ___ browser
9. Memory ___

TIPS II: English-Language News Websites

These are some of the best places online to read about world news.

North American News Sources

Company	Website	Notes
ABC News	abcnews.go.com	U.S. and world news from major American television network
CBS News	www.cbsnews.com	U.S. and world news from major American television network
CNN	www.cnn.com	Major source of U.S. and world news, by subject
Fox News	www.foxnews.com	U.S. and world news from major American television network
Google News	www.google.com/news	U.S. and world news, by subject
MSNBC	www.msnbc.msn.com	U.S. and world news from major American television network

North American Sources Cont.

Company	Website	Notes
New York Post	www.nypost.com	Online edition of important national newspaper
Time / CNN	www.time.com	U.S. and world news, by subject. Includes blogs and archived articles.
U.S. Newswire	releases.usnewswire.com	Current headlines
US News & World Report	www.usnews.com	U.S. and world news, by subject, with special categories (e.g. America's Best)
USA Today	www.usatoday.com	U.S. and world news, by subject, with classifieds, video, archives
Washington Post	www.washingtonpost.com	Online edition of important national newspaper
Yahoo! News	news.yahoo.com	U.S. and world news, by subject

Fill in the vocabulary:

By subject: *Blogs:*

Archived article: *Classifieds:*

Newspapers around the world are now online

European News Sources

Company	Website	Notes
BBC News	news.bbc.co.uk	British and world news from major UK television network
Der Spiegel	www.spiegel.de/spiegel/english	Important German paper offers English translations of some articles
Digital Media Europe	www.dmeurope.com	News by country, mostly on internet and technology
Euobserver.com	euobserver.com	European news, by subject
EuroNews	www.euronews.net	European news, by subject (in many languages)
Guardian Unlimited	www.guardian.co.uk	Somewhat liberal British news source
International Herald Tribune	www.iht.com	Major news source, situated in Paris
Le Monde diplomatique	mondediplo.com	Powerful conservative French news source
RadioFreeEurope	www.rferl.org	News by country and language, with audio
The Independent	news.independent.co.uk/Europe	Important British news source
WN Europe	www.wneurope.com	World news with a European perspective

Liberal: *Conservative:*

Perspective:

News Sources from Asia and Oceania

Company	Website	Notes
ABC News Online	www.abc.net.au/news	Major Australian news agency
Asahi Shimbun	www.asahi.com/english/english.html	Japanese newspaper, online edition
Bangkok Post	www.bangkokpost.com	Excellent resources for ESL students
China Daily	www.chinadaily.com.cn	English-language newspaper
ChinaNews	www.chinanews.cn	Independent national news agency
Daily Yomiuri Online	www.yomiuri.co.jp/dy	Japanese newspaper, online edition
Fuji News Network	www.fnn-news.com/en/index.html	Japanese news with video streams
Kyodo News	home.kyodo.co.jp	Japanese news service
Mainichi Daily news	mdn.mainichi-msn.co.jp	Japanese newspaper, online edition
New Zealand Herald	www.nzherald.co.nz	News from New Zealand and the world
The Australian	www.theaustralian.news.com.au	National Australian news service
The Japan Times Online	www.japantimes.co.jp	Japanese newspaper, online edition
The Korea Herald	www.koreaherald.co.kr	Korean newspaper, online edition
Yonhap News	english.yna.co.kr	South Korean news in English

Streaming video:

Other News Sources

Company	Website	Notes
1st Headlines	www.1stheadlines.com	Newspaper articles from around the world, by subject and region
Headline Spot	www.headlinespot.com	News by subject, region and media (radio, television, magazines)
Newslink	newslink.org	News by region and media, with blogs
Topix.net	www.topix.net/us	U.S. and world news, by subject. Includes forums and blogs.
World Newspapers	www.world-newspapers.com	International newspapers, magazines by topic

With a good grasp of English, you can travel the world

without leaving your living room

 **Famous Saying**

To err is human, to forgive divine.
(Alexander Pope, 1688-1744)

 **Famous Saying**

Garbage in, garbage out (GIGO)
(Anonymous)

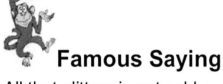 **Famous Saying**

All that glitters is not gold
(Anonymous)

TIPS III: Registration and Logging In

Many sites are free, but require an initial registration for access

Content of a Typical Registration Page

Family Name → If your name is John Smith, your family name is Smith

Given Names → If your name is John Adam Smith, your given names are John and Adam

Address

    Apt → Enter your apartment number, plus the name of the building (e.g. #210 Urban Flats)

    Street → Enter the street address for your building (e.g. 1310 Free Street)

    City → Enter the city where you live (e.g. Chicago)

State	→	Enter the region where you live, or just "NA" (not applicable)
Country	→	Enter your country (e.g. Japan)
Zip Code	→	Enter your postal code (e.g. 762-1111)
Date of Birth	→	Enter the day you were born (e.g. December 1st, 1980 sometimes 01/12/80 or 12/01/80)
Occupation	→	Enter your job (e.g. teacher, student)
Login Name	→	Create a name to use on this site (e.g. sparky813)
Password	→	Create a secret password (e.g. wallflower)

Section 2: Verbs (Part I)

2.1 To add fuel to the fire

Meaning: To make a bad situation even worse; to aggravate a problem

Meaning in your language:

Usage: *A* (person, group) adds fuel to the fire by *B* (action)

1. The prosecutor <u>added fuel to the fire</u> by accusing the witness of committing perjury.

Prosecutor: *Accusing the witness:*

To commit perjury:

2. The way he flirts with his secretary is <u>adding fuel to the fire</u>. I think his wife is going to ask for a divorce.

To flirt: *Divorce:*

3. The death of the automobile passenger may <u>add fuel to the fire</u> regarding seatbelt legislation.

Automobile passenger: *Seatbelt legislation:*

Related expressions: To make matters worse

                                  To add insult to injury

2.2 (To bear) the brunt of criticism

Meaning: To be criticized, or to suffer

Meaning in your language:

Usage: *A* (person, group) bears the brunt of *B* (criticism)

1. The regional manager for the company <u>bore the brunt of the criticism</u> from the labor union.

Regional manager: *Labor union:*

2. The train driver <u>bore the brunt of criticism</u> for the derailment.

Train driver: *Derailment:*

3. The <u>brunt of</u> the inspector's <u>criticism</u> was directed at the owners of the pharmaceutical factory.

Inspector: *Directed at:*

Pharmaceutical factory:

Related expressions: The lion's share

                                  The scapegoat

2.3 To blow the whistle on

Meaning: To report something (bad) to the newspapers, police, etc.

Meaning in your language:

Usage: *A* (person) blows the whistle on *B* (action)

1. The chairperson was fired after his secretary <u>blew the whistle on</u> his bribe-taking.

Chairperson: *Fired:*   *Bribe-taking:*

2. The report <u>blew the whistle on</u> the company's illegal trading operations with impoverished countries.

Illegal trading: *Impoverished:*

3. He received a lot of attention after <u>blowing the whistle on</u> the unsanitary conditions at the restaurant.

To receive attention: *Unsanitary conditions:*

Related expressions: To rat on
                                  To leak

2.4 To brace (for)

Meaning: To prepare for something difficult

Meaning in your language:

Usage: *A* (person group) braces for *B* (future event)

1. The weather forecaster said that we should <u>brace</u> ourselves <u>for</u> a week of sub-zero temperatures.

Weather forecaster: *Sub-zero temperatures:*

2. The employees <u>braced</u> themselves <u>for</u> layoffs following the news that the company was closing some of its stores.

Layoffs: *Closing stores:*

3. The pilot said, "<u>Brace</u> yourselves!" just before the plane crashed.

Pilot:

Related expressions: To prepare for
                                  To steel oneself

2.5 To break out

Meaning #1: To occur (often something bad such as a war, disease or fire)

Meaning in your language:

Usage: *A* (bad situation) breaks out

1. The fire at the abandoned factory <u>broke out</u> just after 6 am this morning.

Abandoned factory:

2. War <u>will</u> probably <u>break out</u> soon if these boarder skirmishes continue.

Boarder skirmishes:

Meaning #2: To escape (from jail)

Meaning in your language:

1. The prisoner <u>broke out</u> of the maximum security prison late last night.

Prisoner: *Maximum security prison:*

2. Don't even think about trying <u>to break out</u>. The guards use specially trained Dobermans.

Specially trained: *Dobermans:*

Related expressions: To erupt (Meaning #1)

To fly the coop (Meaning #2)

There are concerns that war may break out

2.6 To brush aside

Meaning: To ignore something (usually criticism)

Meaning in your language:

Usage: *A* (person) brushes aside *B* (criticism)
1. The police commissioner <u>brushed aside</u> questions from the press regarding the homicide inquiry.
Police commissioner: *Homicide:*   *Inquiry:*
2. The overworked executive <u>brushed aside</u> concerns regarding his health.
Overworked: *Executive:*
Concerns regarding:
3. All thoughts of personal safety were <u>brushed aside</u> as the neighbors worked together to repair the breach in the dam.
Personal safety: *Dam:*
Repair the breach:

Related expressions: Leave aside

Cast a blind eye

2.7 To burn the midnight oil

Meaning: To work hard; to study late into the night

Meaning in your language:

Usage: *A* (person) burns the midnight oil because of *B* (deadline, project)
1. If you keep <u>burning the midnight oil</u>, you are going to make yourself sick.
To make oneself sick:
2. The students had <u>to burn the midnight oil</u> in order to pass their entrance exams.
Entrance exams:
3. The team is <u>burning the midnight oil</u>, training weeks in advance for the semi-finals.
In advance: *Semi-finals:*

Related expressions: To burn the candle at both ends

To work like a dog

2.8 To carve out a niche in

Meaning: To become successful in some field

Meaning in your language:

Usage: *A* (person, group) carves out a niche in *B* (field)

1. She is carving out a niche in the highly male-dominated business world.

Male-dominated: *Business world:*

2. The up and coming painter says that his goal is to carve out a niche in the art world.

Up and coming painter: *Art world:*

3. That jewelry store tried to carve out a niche in the local consumer market, but failed.

Jewelry store: *Local consumer market:*

Failed:

Related expressions: To make a name for oneself

                                  To find a place

2.9 To cast a pall over

Meaning: To raise doubts about something; to question the authority of something; to ruin something

Meaning in your language:

Usage: *A* (person, group) casts a pall on *B* (person, group, situation)

1. The drug-taking incident has cast a pall over the Olympic opening ceremonies.

Drug-taking: *Opening ceremonies:*

2. Her poor behavior has cast a pall over the reputation of the committee.

Reputation: *Committee:*

3. Allegations of kickbacks have cast a pall over the entire legal system.

Allegations: *Kickbacks:*   *Legal system:*

Related expressions: A shadow of doubt over

                                  To tarnish the reputation of

2.10 To cause a stir

Meaning: To start a debate; to make trouble; to be the center of attention
Meaning in your language:

> **Usage**:   *A* (person, group) causes a stir by *B* (action)
>
> 1. The new designer <u>is causing</u> quite <u>a stir</u> in the fashion industry with her avant-garde styles.
>
> *Designer:*   *Fashion industry:*   *Avant-garde:*
>
> 2. The fast food chain <u>caused</u> quite <u>a stir</u> by offering free hamburgers as part of their 50th anniversary celebrations.
>
> *Fast food chain:*   *Anniversary celebration:*
>
> 3. News of the wiretapping by the police <u>has caused</u> quite <u>a stir</u> among civil rights groups.
>
> *Wiretapping:*   *Civil rights groups:*

Related expressions: To stir up a hornet's nest
                                     To stir up controversy (See 2.78)

2.11 To charge with

Meaning: To formally accuse someone of a crime (legal vocabulary)
Meaning in your language:

> **Usage**:   *A* (person) is charged with *B* (crime)
>
>   *A* (person) charges *B* (person) with *C* (crime)
>
> 1. The federal detectives finally <u>charged</u> him <u>with</u> the murder of his wife.
>
> *Federal detectives:*   *Murder:*
>
> 2. The CEO may be <u>charged with</u> stealing money from the operating budget.
>
> *CEO:*   *Operating budget:*
>
> 3. If she <u>is charged with</u> drunk driving, she will probably lose her license.
>
> *Drunk driving:*   *License:*

Related expressions: Sent up the river
                                     To press charges

2.12 To cite

Meaning: To give examples, showing evidence to support your belief

Meaning in your language:

Usage: *A* (decision, argument), citing *B* (example)

1. The university has closed its extension campus, <u>citing</u> the decline in demand in recent years.

Extension campus: *Decline in demand:*

2. The cabinet minister said that he has the support of the people, <u>citing</u> recent opinion polls.

Cabinet minister: *Support of the people:*

Opinion polls:

3. <u>Citing</u> a recent national survey on smoking and health, the airline has decided to ban smoking on all flights.

National survey: *Airline:*

To ban smoking:

Related expressions: To finger

To draw on

2.13 To clamp down on

Meaning: To treat some behavior seriously; to prohibit something

Meaning in your language:

Usage: *A* (group) clamps down on *B* (activity)

1. The police <u>are clamping down on</u> the illegal parking of bicycles.

Illegal parking of bicycles:

2. That upscale coffee shop <u>is</u> really <u>clamping down on</u> people who smoke in the non-smoking section.

Upscale: *Non-smoking section:*

3. I wish the federal government would <u>clamp down on</u> citizens who cheat on their income tax.

Federal government: *Cheat on income tax:*

Related expressions: To crack down on (See 2.16)

To stamp out

60

2.14 To clean up one's act

Meaning: To improve oneself; to study harder; to act correctly

Meaning in your language:

Usage: *A* (person) should clean up his/her act

1. The school board representative will really need <u>to clean up</u> his <u>act</u> if he wants to be re-elected next term.

School board: *Representative:*

2. If that sophomore student doesn't <u>clean up</u> her <u>act</u>, she's going to be expelled.

Sophomore: *Expelled:*

3. <u>Clean up</u> your <u>act</u> or there will be no chance of getting a year-end bonus.

Year-end bonus:

Related expressions: To know one's stuff

To get it together

2.15 To cost someone

Meaning: To lose something or fail because of some action/behavior

Meaning in your language:

Usage: *A* (action) costs *B* (person, group) *C* (some goal)

1. The president's controversial support for communist groups may <u>have cost him</u> the election.

Controversial support: *Communist groups:*

Election:

2. Her lack of punctuality <u>will</u> probably <u>cost her</u> the examination.

Punctuality: *(School) examination:*

3. The rude response by the regional manager <u>will</u> surely <u>cost the company</u> a number of customers.

Rude response: *Regional manager:*

Related expressions: To forfeit something

To screw something up

2.16 To crack down (a crackdown) on

Meaning: The government or the police are working hard to stop something illegal

Meaning in your language:

Usage: *A* (police, government) cracks down on *B* (illegal behavior)

1. There has been a <u>crack down</u> recently <u>on</u> littering in parks in the downtown area.

Littering:　　　　　　　　*Downtown area:*

2. The police said that they <u>will be cracking down on</u> drunk drivers during the holidays.

Drunk drivers:　　　　　　　*During the holidays:*

3. The women's shelter said that <u>a crackdown on</u> domestic violence is needed.

Women's shelter:　　　　　　*Domestic violence:*

Related expressions:　　　　To get tough on

　　　　　　　　　　　　　　To clamp down on (see 2.13)

Police are cracking down on illegal gambling

2.17 To credit ... to

Meaning: To thank someone or something for your success

Meaning in your language:

Usage: *A* (person) credits *B* (good fortune) to *C* (action, person, force)

1. The old man <u>credits</u> his longevity <u>to</u> his habit of drinking one glass of sherry every day.

Longevity: *Sherry:*

2. She <u>credited</u> her splendid showing at the Olympics <u>to</u> her many years of hard work.

Splendid showing: *Years of hard work:*

3. The actor <u>credits</u> his successful career <u>to</u> his choice of movie roles.

Actor: *Career:*   *Movie roles:*

Related expressions: To owe it all to

To chalk it up to

2.18 To dawn on

Meaning: To suddenly understand; to realize

Meaning in your language:

Usage: *A* (fact) dawns on *B* (person)

1. It suddenly <u>dawned on</u> the translator that he could be more successful working freelance.

Translator: *To work freelance:*

Working freelance:

2. After a year of marriage it <u>dawned on</u> her that her husband had only married her for her money.

For money:

3. The seriousness of his brush with law only <u>dawned on</u> him many weeks later.

Seriousness: *Brush with the law:*

Related expressions: The other shoe dropped

To sink in (See 2.72)

2.19 To dismiss (as)

Meaning: To criticize something; to think that something is not important

Meaning in your language:

Usage: *A* (action, situation, object, person) is dismissed as *B* (judgment) by *C* (person)

1. The formal apology for his racist remarks <u>was dismissed</u> by the media <u>as</u> too little, too late.

Formal apology: *Racist remark:*   *Media:*

2. The staff member was criticized by his manager <u>for dismissing</u> the customer's complaint.

Staff member: *Customer's complaint:*

3. The millionaire recluse <u>dismissed the</u> report of his serious illness <u>as</u> just a rumor.

Recluse: *Serious illness:*

Related expressions: To discredit
                                              To ignore

He dismissed my idea to get some exercise

2.20 To dog

Meaning: To make trouble for someone; to follow someone wherever they go

Meaning in your language:

Usage: **A** (person, group) is dogged by **B** (person, group)

1. He has a lot of problems because his criminal record <u>dogs</u> him every time he applies for a new job.

Criminal record: *To apply for a job:*

2. That poor politician <u>is dogged</u> by questions about her private life.

Private life:

3. The tobacco company spokesperson <u>is dogged</u> by antismoking protestors wherever he goes.

Tobacco company: *Spokesperson:*

Antismoking protestors:

Related expressions: To haunt

                                 To shadow

2.21 To draw attention to

Meaning: To make people see something; to focus or talk about something

Meaning in your language:

Usage: **A** (person, group) draws attention to **B** (fact, situation)

1. He <u>drew attention to</u> the poor living conditions by inviting newspaper reporters to inspect the tenement.

Poor living conditions: *Newspaper reporters:*

To inspect: *Tenement:*

2. The neighborhood association is hoping <u>to draw</u> public <u>attention to</u> the dangers of bicycling while carrying a young child.

Neighborhood   *Association:*

3. His mission is to <u>draw attention to</u> the dangers of nuclear weapons.

Mission: *Nuclear weapons:*

Related expressions: To underscore

                                 To hammer home

2.22 To draw criticism (from)

Meaning: To be criticized by someone, or by a group of people

Meaning in your language:

Usage: **A** (person, group, action) draws criticism from **B** (person, group)

1. The mayor <u>has drawn criticism from</u> the African American community for his latest speech.

African American community:

2. The plan to build a hydroelectric dam in the nature reserve <u>has drawn criticism from</u> a variety of people.

Hydroelectric dam: *Nature reserve:*

A variety of people:

3. The fledgling actor <u>drew criticism</u> for his poor performance in the play.

Fledgling actor: *Poor performance:*

Related expressions: To be under fire

                                               To be on the hot seat

The laboratory is drawing criticism for its safety policy

2.23 To erupt in(to)

Meaning: To do something forcefully or suddenly

Meaning in your language:

Usage: *A* (person, group) erupts in *B* (action)

1. The crowd <u>erupted in</u> applause when the movie star arrived outside the hotel.

Crowd: *Applause:*   *Movie star:*

2. The war of words between the two countries <u>may erupt into</u> violence very soon.

War of words:

3. The senators <u>erupted in</u> laughter when the president fell off the podium.

Senators: *Podium:*

Related expressions: A flashpoint

                                     To burst into

2.24 To eye

Meaning: To be attracted to something or someone

Meaning in your language:

Usage: *A* (person) eyes *B* (something interesting)

1. The company <u>is eyeing</u> a piece of land just south of the city as the site for its new factory.

Piece of land: *Factory site:*

2. The boy <u>eyed</u> the gingerbread candy on the Christmas tree even though it was almost time for dinner.

Gingerbread:

3. He keeps <u>eyeing</u> that new red sports car in the showroom window.

Sports car: *Showroom window:*

Related expressions: To check out

                                       With an eye to

2.25 To face (up to)

Meaning: To expect and/or prepare for some problem; to be honest about past mistakes

Meaning in your language:

Usage: *A* (person, group) faces up to *B* (problem)

1. The drunk driver decided <u>to face</u> the angry mob rather than trying to hide.

Drunk driver: *Angry mob:*

2. The high school principal <u>faced up to</u> his mistake and apologized to the head of the PTA.

To apologize: *PTA (Parent-Teacher Association):*

Cutbacks:

3. The deputy minister's plan to raise taxes <u>is facing</u> strong opposition from the public.

Deputy minister: *Opposition:*

Related Expression: To face the music

To run into (see 2.66)

2.26 To fall on deaf ears

Meaning: To ignore something; to refuse a request

Meaning in your language:

Usage: *A* (action, news, request) falls on deaf ears

1. It is not surprising that the supermarket is doing poorly, because consumer complaints always <u>fall on deaf ears</u> there.

Supermarket: *Consumer complaints:*

2. Her ideas for product improvement <u>fell on deaf ears</u> because her company is very conservative.

Product improvement: *Conservative:*

3. Public opinion <u>fell on deaf ears</u> as the unpopular antiterrorism bill became law.

Public opinion: *Antiterrorism bill:*

To become law:

Related expressions: To get the cold shoulder

Like talking to a brick wall

2.27 To fall through

Meaning: Something looked hopeful, but failed to happen.

Meaning in your language:

Usage: *A* (contract, agreement, plans) falls through because of *B* (reason)

1. The plans to redevelop the harbor area <u>fell through</u> after protests from the warehouse companies.

To redevelop: *Harbor area:*

Warehouse companies:

2. He started drinking to excess after his marriage plans <u>fell through</u>.

To drink to excess: *Marriage plans:*

3. The movie studio said that talks with the writer <u>fell through</u> because she wanted too much money.

Movie studio: *Talks with the writer:*

Related expressions: To hit the skids

                                    To fail to materialize

Unfortunately, his plans for a vacation fell through

2.28 To fence in

Meaning: To hold or trap someone; to give them too much attention
Meaning in your language:

Usage: *A* (person, group) fences in *B* (person)

1. She left the marriage because she felt <u>fenced in</u> by her husband.
Left the marriage:

2. Don't <u>fence</u> your son <u>in</u>! Teenagers need the opportunity to develop their independence.
Teenagers: *Opportunity:*   *Independence:*

3. The celebrity's husband said he felt <u>fenced in</u> by all the paparazzi and their questions.
Celebrity: *Paparazzi:*

Related expressions: To corner someone
To feel put upon

2.29 To follow in (the footsteps of)

Meaning: To copy someone or something else
Meaning in your language:

Usage: *A* (action, situation) follows in the footsteps of *B* (action, situation)

1. The singer is going <u>to follow in the footsteps of</u> his idol, Elvis, and someday become a superstar.
Singer: *Idol:*   *Superstar:*

2. That coffee shop <u>is following in the footsteps of</u> the major department stores by offering free delivery during the holidays.
Coffee shop: *Free delivery:*   *The holidays:*

3. He <u>followed in</u> his brother's <u>footsteps</u> and entered art college.
Art college:

Related expressions: To ape
To stand on the shoulders of

2.30 To gain momentum

Meaning: Some activity is becoming more common.

Meaning in your language:

Usage: *A* (activity) is gaining momentum

1. The peace talks <u>are gaining momentum</u>, and there may be a diplomatic solution in a few days.

Peace talks: *Diplomatic solution:*

2. There's no question that use of the internet <u>has gained momentum</u>, especially among young people.

3. The idea of "flex time" <u>is gaining momentum</u>, and our company may introduce it soon.

Flex time:

Related expressions: To pick up steam

To get one's stride

2.31 To (not) let someone get a word in edgewise

Meaning: You want to say something, but your partner is talking too much.

Meaning in your language:

Usage: *A* (person) can't get a word in edgewise

1. I wanted to explain my behavior, but he wouldn't <u>let</u> me <u>get a word in edgewise</u>.

To explain my behavior:

2. If you'd <u>let</u> me <u>get a word in edgewise</u>, I'd tell you where I was all night.

3. The corporate representative would <u>not let</u> the researchers <u>get a word in edgewise</u> at the news conference.

Corporate representative: *Researchers:*

News conference:

Related expressions: To have your say

To be a motor-mouth

2.32 To get burned

Meaning: To have a bad experience with something

Meaning in your language:

Usage: *A* (person) gets burned by *B* (person, situation)

1. He really <u>got burned</u> on the stock market a few years ago. He lost all his savings.

Stock market: *Savings:*

2. The presidential candidate <u>got burned</u> in the primaries because his views on abortion were unpopular.

Presidential candidate: *Primaries:*

Abortion:

3. She <u>got burned</u> in the divorce settlement, and is afraid of ever marrying again.

Divorce settlement:

Related expressions: To get taken for a ride
                                                 To lose one's shirt

He got burned by the greedy real estate agent

2.33 To get caught up

Meaning #1: To share stories with someone you haven't seen for a long time

Meaning in your language:

Usage: *A* (person) and *B* (person) get caught up over *C* (occasion)

1. My old college friend and I <u>got caught up</u> over lunch yesterday.

College friend:

2. Let's <u>get caught up</u> sometime - you can tell me about your marriage and your new house.

Meaning #2: Finish homework, housework, or projects at work

Meaning in your language:

1. I don't think I'll ever <u>get caught up</u> with this mountain of homework for my psychology class!

Mountain of homework: *Psychology class:*

2. My children keep me so busy that I never seem to <u>get caught up</u> with the housework.

Housework:

Related expressions: To chew the fat (Meaning #1)

To tie up loose ends (Meaning #2)

2.34 To get off scot free

Meaning: To escape punishment

Meaning in your language:

Usage: *A* (person, group) gets off scot free

1. There was no incriminating evidence against him, so he <u>got off scot free</u>.

Incriminating evidence:

2. The accused <u>will</u> probably <u>get off scot free</u> because of his expensive lawyer.

The accused: *Expensive lawyer:*

3. Even though he is an influential person in the business world, I don't think he <u>will get off scot free</u>.

Influential person: *Business world:*

Related expressions: A narrow escape

To emerge unscathed

2.35 To get on the bandwagon

Meaning: To join the majority; to agree with current opinion

Meaning in your language:

Usage: *A* (person, group) gets on the bandwagon

1. Many well-known fundraisers <u>got on the bandwagon</u> to elect Obama in 2008.

Fundraisers: *To elect:*

2. Many people <u>are getting on</u> the recycling <u>bandwagon</u> by bringing their milk cartons back to the supermarket.

Recycling: *Milk cartons:*

3. She <u>got on the</u> "clean up the city" <u>bandwagon</u> by volunteering to pick up trash in the streets.

Pick up trash:

Related expressions: To rubber-stamp

To chime in

2.36 To get the ball rolling

Meaning: To begin some project; to encourage others to begin something

Meaning in your language:

Usage: *A* (person, group) gets the ball rolling by *B* (action)

1. He <u>got the ball rolling</u> on environmental issues by signing the new anti-pollution law.

Environmental issues: *Anti-pollution law:*

2. I <u>got the ball rolling</u> on my job search by writing up my resume.

Job search: *Resume:*

3. The director <u>got the ball rolling</u> on the new movie by having each of the actors do a walk-through.

Director: *Walk-through:*

Related expressions: To kick things off

To start things off

2.37 To give a green light to

Meaning: To approve something; to proceed with or continue something

Meaning in your language:

Usage: **A** (person, group) gives a green light to **B** (project)

1. The Ministry of Transport <u>has given the green light to</u> the restructuring of the national railway.

Ministry of Transport: *Restructuring:*

National railway:

2. The planning agency <u>has given the green light to</u> the redevelopment project.

Planning agency: *Redevelopment:*

3. I met with my boss, and he <u>gave me the green light to</u> proceed with my ideas.

To proceed with:

Related expressions: To ok something

                                          To rubber stamp something

The new project has been given the green light

2.38 To give someone the benefit of the doubt

Meaning: To have faith in someone; to trust someone even though their story sounds false

Meaning in your language:

Usage: *A* (person, group) gives *B* (person, group) the benefit of the doubt

1. The record company decided <u>to give</u> the fledgling group <u>the benefit of the doubt</u>, and offered them a contract.

Record company: *Fledgling group:*

A contract:

2. Please <u>give</u> me <u>the benefit of the doubt</u> - I swear that I am innocent of these allegations.

To swear (that):   *Innocent:*   *Allegations:*

3. The company said that they couldn't <u>give</u> him <u>the benefit of the doubt</u> because he was caught red-handed with the store ledger.

Red-handed: *Ledger:*

Related expressions: To turn the other check

To turn a blind eye to

2.39 To give someone the slip

Meaning: To escape from something or someone

Meaning in your language:

Usage: *A* (person) gives *B* (person) the slip

1. The criminal <u>gave</u> the police <u>the slip</u> by wearing women's clothing.

Criminal: *Women's clothing:*

2. The student <u>gave</u> the teacher <u>the slip</u> by hiding in the locker room.

Hiding: *Locker room:*

3. The frantic mother called the department store security guards after her little boy <u>gave</u> her <u>the slip</u>.

Frantic: *Department store:*

Security guards:

Related expressions: To evade

To lose track of

2.40 To give way to

Meaning: Something (such as mood or public opinion) changes or reverses.

Meaning in your language:

Usage: *A* (mood, opinion) gives way to *B* (mood, opinion)

1. The sense of elation following his election soon gave way to disappointment with his new policies.

Sense of elation: *Disappointment:*

New policies:

2. The team's sadness over the loss of the important game has given way to determination to win next time.

Determination:

3. Public interest in the tabloid story has finally given way to boredom.

Tabloid story: *Boredom:*

Related expressions: The tide has turned

                                 The morning after

2.41 To go into effect

Meaning: To become policy or law

Meaning in your language:

Usage: *A* (law, policy) goes into effect at *B* (time)

1. The new speed limit for residential districts goes into effect at midnight tomorrow.

Speed limit: *Residential districts:*

2. Even if the new law against graft goes into effect, I doubt the police will be able to enforce it.

Graft: *To enforce:*

3. The no-smoking policy at the company is expected to go into effect by January of next year.

No-smoking policy:

Related expressions: To become policy

                                 To sign into law

2.42 To have a run-in with

Meaning: To have an unfortunate meeting with someone or something (a fight)
Meaning in your language:

Usage: **A** (person, group) has a run-in with **B** (person, group)
1. I <u>had a run-in with</u> his wife and I felt embarrassed when I saw him again.
To feel embarrassed:
2. The homeless person <u>had a run-in with</u> the police, who didn't want him sleeping in the park.
Homeless person:
3. She decided to change jobs after numerous <u>run-ins with</u> her obnoxious coworker.
Numerous: *Obnoxious:*   *Coworker:*

Related expressions: To lock horns with
                              To have a tiff

2.43 To have no alternative but to

Meaning: To do something because there is no other choice
Meaning in your language:

Usage: **A** (person, group) has no alternative but to **B** (action)
1. The roads are closed because of the heavy snow, so I <u>have no alternative but to</u> stay home.
Closed roads: *Heavy snow:*   *Stay home:*
2. Because of the serious condition of the plane crash survivor, the doctor <u>had no alternative but to</u> operate.
Plane crash survivor: *Serious condition:*
To operate:
3. She was rude to the customers and was always late for work. I <u>had no alternative but to</u> fire her.
Rude to customers: *Late for work:*   *To fire:*

Related expressions: Had no choice but to....
                              Hands are tied

2.44 To have ties to

Meaning: To have connections with some person or group

Meaning in your language:

Usage: *A* (person, group) has ties to *B* (person, group)

1. Be careful! I'm sure he <u>has ties to</u> the mafia.

Mafia:

2. The police are investigating the company's <u>ties to</u> the banned religious cult.

To investigate: *Banned religious cult:*

3. He gets invited everywhere because of his <u>ties to</u> royalty and the aristocracy

To be invited everywhere:

Royalty and the aristocracy:

Related expressions: In bed with

Thick as thieves

2.45 To keep an eye on

Meaning: To watch; to guard; to be careful of something

Meaning in your language:

Usage: *A* (person) keeps an eye on *B* (person, situation)

1. The stockholders are <u>keeping an eye on</u> the IPO after rumors of a merger hit the internet.

Stockholder: *IPO (Initial Public Offering):*

Merger:

2. We should <u>keep an eye on</u> that mole. If it continues to grow you will need an operation.

Mole: Operation:

3. The Minister of Finance <u>is keeping an eye on</u> the inflation rate and may intervene if the economy doesn't improve.

Inflation rate: *Intervene:*   *Economy:*

Related expressions: To keep one's eyes peeled

To be on the lookout for

2.46 To leave… (to / with)

Meaning: To give someone the responsibility for something

Meaning in your language:

Usage: *A* (person, group) leaves *B* (some action) to/with C (some person, group)

1. <u>Leave it with</u> me. I will take care of the paperwork for you.

Paperwork:

2. We can't just <u>leave</u> environmental protection <u>to</u> the government, because it's everyone's responsibility.

Environmental protection: *Responsibility:*

3. I wouldn't <u>leave it with</u> him - he seems awfully unreliable.

To seem: *Unreliable:*

Related expressions: Take the ball and run with it

The ball is in one's court

2.47 To lie ahead

Meaning: To talk about what is coming in the future

Meaning in your language:

Usage: *A* (event) lies ahead for *B* (person)

1. I have no idea what <u>lies ahead</u> in my life, and I certainly don't worry about it.

To worry about:

2. If I had known what <u>was lying ahead</u>, I would have sold my shares in the company before the recession.

Shares: *Recession:*

3. It was great to get the funding, but a lot of research now <u>lies ahead</u>.

Funding: *Research:*

Related expressions: In the cards (See 3.38)

Down the road

Mini-Quiz: Verbs Part I

Part A

1.Get ready to.... another long, cold winter in Sapporo.

a) go into effect   **b)** face   **c)** get the ball rolling   **d)** dog

2.The police plan to ..... drunk driving over the holidays.

a) fall through   **b)** crack down on   **c)** dawn on   **d)** give a green light to

3.It's very hard.... when I'm having coffee with my wife.

a) to get a word in edgewise   **b)** to fall through   **c)** go into effect   **d)** to credit

4.He .... as a pianist to his years of classical musical training.

a) causes a stir   **b)** credits his success   **c)** brushes aside   **d)** faces up to

5.According to the satellite images, we should all .... a typhoon.

a) brace for   **b)** have ties to   **c)** leave it to   **d)** get burned

6.If the prime minister doesn't start ..... he could lose his job.

a) cleaning up his act   **b)** drawing criticism   **c)** dogging   **d)** giving someone the slip

7.His bad behavior at the press conference.... the election.

a) braced for   **b)** get burned   **c)** leave with   **d)** cost him

8. Laughing at the boss when he criticized me only...
a) had ties with   **b)** dismissed as   **c)** fell on deaf ears   **d)** added fuel to the fire

9. Experts fear that the recent clashes at the border may .... full-scale war.
a) cast a pall over   **b)** add fuel to the fire   **c)** break out   **d)** erupt into

10. His press secretary ... on his scandalous behavior.
a) blew the whistle on **b)** drew attention **c)** followed in **d)** started the ball rolling

11. The Moslem community's request for support from City Hall …
a) got burned   **b)** fell on deaf ears   **c)** got on the bandwagon   **d)** lie ahead

12. Plans for a nationwide chain of private clinics…
a) broke out   **b)** cited   **c)** gives way   **d)** fell through

13. … you stress level and take more breaks during the day.
a) Keep an eye on   **b)** Leave it to   **c)** Fence in   **d)** Erupt into

14. Buy our life insurance: you never know what …
a) gives someone the slip   **b)** goes into effect   **c)** lies ahead   **d)** gets burned

15. All of the spectators … the excitement of the home run.
a) got caught up in   **b)** fell through   **c)** drew criticism from   **d)** drew attention to

Part B

1. To have		**a.** attention to
2. To draw		**b.** eye on
3. To burn		**c.** the slip
4. To get a word		**d.** a pall over
5. To add		**e.** in edgewise
6. To gain		**f.** the midnight oil
7. To cast		**g.** on
8. To fall on		**h.** through
9. To give a		**i.** green light to
10. To dawn		**j.** ball rolling
11. To give someone		**k.** momentum
12. To fall		**l.** down on
13. To clamp		**m.** deaf ears
14. To keep an		**n.** fuel to the fire
15. To get the		**o.** ties to

Part C

E.g. may / that / as / be / it : <u>Be that as it may</u>

1. fuel / fire / to / to / add / the   : _____
2. to / the / on / blow / whistle   : _____
3. to / burn / oil / the / midnight   : _____
4. in / niche / a / out / carve / to   : _____
5. a / on / pall / cast / to   : _____
6. to / stir / a / cause   : _____
7. to / down / clamp / on   : _____
8. up / one's / act / to / clean   : _____
9. down / crack / to / on   : _____
10. to / to / attention / draw   : _____

Her wedding announcement really caused a stir (see 2.13)

TIPS IV: Understanding Online News Articles

A) <u>Basic Structure of a News Article</u>

Most articles have are built from the following primary elements:

1) Headline ⟶

2) By-line

3) Lead (1st sentence/sometimes 1st paragraph)

4) Body and Final Paragraph

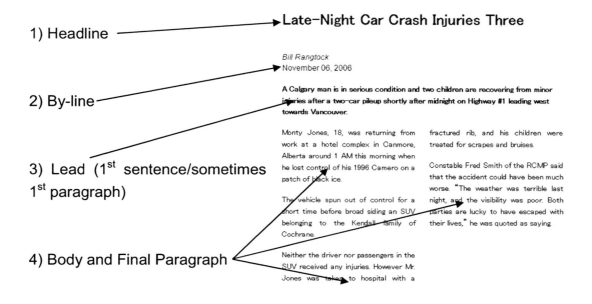

Late-Night Car Crash Injuries Three

Bill Rangtock
November 06, 2006

A Calgary man is in serious condition and two children are recovering from minor injuries after a two-car pileup shortly after midnight on Highway #1 leading west towards Vancouver.

Monty Jones, 18, was returning from work at a hotel complex in Canmore, Alberta around 1 AM this morning when he lost control of his 1996 Camero on a patch of black ice.

The vehicle spun out of control for a short time before broad siding an SUV belonging to the Kendall family of Cochrane.

Neither the driver nor passengers in the SUV received any injuries. However Mr. Jones was taken to hospital with a fractured rib, and his children were treated for scrapes and bruises.

Constable Fred Smith of the RCMP said that the accident could have been much worse. "The weather was terrible last night, and the visibility was poor. Both parties are lucky to have escaped with their lives," he was quoted as saying.

B) Features of Headlines

1) Headlines are often about current events, and involve topical themes.

[TIP: Articles are easier to understand if you read the news often, and are familiar with current events. Do some background reading.]

2) Headlines often use special vocabulary, with a focus on short and colorful words.

Here is some typically colorful headline vocabulary:

Vocabulary	Your Language	Sample Headline
Strikes		**Influenza Strikes Town** *Influenza:*
Soars		**Gas Prices Soar**
Blasts		**PM Blasts Opposition Leader** *PM:* *Opposition Leader:*
Fades		**Hopes Fade for Missing Person** *Hope:* *Missing Person:*
Poised to		**Plant Manager Poised To Resign** *Plant Manager:* *Resign:*
Engulfs		**Snowstorm Engulfs Midwest** *Snowstorm:* *Midwest:*
Wins		**Smith Wins Nomination** *Nomination:*
Loses		**Johnson Loses Presidency** *Presidency:*
Cuts		**Pay Cuts Expected** *Pay cuts:*

2.1) Headlines often make use of pop references and neologisms.

E.g. **Workplace Wars: The Rift Between Gen X and Gen Y**

Gen X (generation X) = people born after the post WWII baby boom

Gen Y (generation Y) = people born from the mid 70s to the mid 90s

E.g. **Brangelina Leave Africa**

Brangelina = Brad Pitt + Angelina Jolie

E.g. **Techno-Savvy Teens More Common: Survey**

Techno-savvy = familiar with/comfortable with technology

3) Headlines have their own special grammar.

-Omission of articles, some verbs

-Preference for present infinitive, present simple, or present passive, even for past events

Try reading and understanding this typical headline:

Element	Content
Headline	**Tax Cut Welcome News for Middle Class–Report**
Current Events (from reading other news articles)	The government reduced taxes recently.
Vocabulary	*A tax cut: (See 1.8)* *Welcome news*: *Middle-class*:
Grammar	A report has shown that many middle-class people are happy about the recent tax cut by the government.

C) <u>Strategies for Reading Headlines</u>

<u>I. Read about current events.</u>
-Research the topic, and understand current events.
-Read any related articles from the past few days.
Topic: *Related articles:*

<u>II. Check the vocabulary.</u>

<u>III. Write the full sentence.</u>
-Fill in the missing words.

<u>IV. Use the headline to understand the article.</u>
-Guess the 5 W's [who, what, where, when, why].
-Check your guesses after reading the article.

Now let's apply these strategies to a sample headline:

Katrina Hits Hard

I. Read about current events.	Katrina is the name of a tropical storm in the southern United States. *Tropical storm:*
II. Check the vocabulary.	*Katrina = Name of a hurricane* *To hit:* *Hard:*
III. Write the full sentence.	Hurricane Katrina has hit New Orleans, and it has caused a lot of damage.
IV. Use the headline to understand the article.	Who = People in New Orleans What = Storm damage Where = New Orleans When = Recently Why = Natural disaster

D) <u>The By-line</u>

The by-line is a single line (after the headline). It gives us some or all of the following information:

Cardiac Care System Insufficient

1) Reporter
2) News agency
3) Local office
4) Date

Jeffry Taylor, Info World, Vancouver, November 06, 2006

Cardiac care at major Canadian hospitals is insufficient to handle the current load, and the problem is only going to get worse, says leading experts.

An expert with the city review board on health care broached this opinion at a press conference held in downtown Vancouver on Wednesday.

Betty Deven said that unless something is done to increase the resources available for hospital care, there will be a crisis at some point in the next decade.

In response to the report, mayor Didsbury pledged to increase the amount of funding allocated to improving the quality of services at hospitals and municipal clinics. No timetable was given, and the amount of funding remains a matter of speculation.

E.g. Reuters, Tokyo, Ken Ichikawa, Tuesday April 15, 2005

Here are some of the largest news agencies:

Agency	Location	Website
Associated Press, The	New York	www.ap.org
Bloomberg, L.P.	New York	www.bloomberg.com
British Broadcasting Corporation	London	www.bbc.co.uk
Canadian Press, The	Canada	www.cp.org
Independent Television News	London	www.itn.co.uk
Kyodo News	Tokyo	home.kyodo.co.jp
Information Telegraph Agency of Russia	Moscow	www.tass.ru/eng
Reuters Group plc	London	reuters.com
United Press International	Washington	www.upi.com

E) <u>The Lead</u>

1) The lead condenses the most important information in an article.

2) The lead focuses on the 5 Ws [who what where when why].

3) It is written in order of interest, not chronological order.

Cardiac Care System Insufficient

Jerry Taylor, Info World, Vancouver, November 06, 2006

Cardiac care at major Canadian hospitals is insufficient to handle the and the problem is only going to get worse, says leading experts.

An expert with the city review board on health care broached this opinion at a press conference held in downtown Vancouver on Wednesday.

Betty Deven said that unless something is done to increase the resources available for hospital care, there will be a crisis at some point in the next decade.

In response to the r Didsbury pledged to increa of funding allocated to quality of services at municipal clinics. No timet: and the amount of fund matter of speculation.

Understanding the Lead

Style	Content
Chronological order	Yesterday I went for a walk in the park. I stopped and ate my lunch. Then I saw a motorcycle crash into a car. The two cyclists were hurt. An ambulance came and took them away.
Lead style	Two people were seriously injured yesterday afternoon when their motorcycle hit an SUV at the corner of Main and Center streets. They were taken by ambulance to the local hospital for treatment of compound fractures.

Style: *Motorcycle:*

To crash into something: *Ambulance:*

SUV: *Serious injuries:*

Compound fractures:

F) Strategies for Reading the Lead

I. Prepare
-Read the headline and find out the background to the story.
Background:

II. Understand the basic grammar
-What is the subject?
-What is the verb?
-What is the object?
-Are there several subjects, or several verbs?

III. Clarify the details
-Make a chart of 5W + H (how) and fill in the answers.

Let's try this strategy with a typical lead:

Section	Content
Headline	**UN Seeks Aid for Central Asia**
Lead	The UN is seeking cooperation from member countries in cleanup efforts following torrential rains across much of Central Asia.
I. Prepare	*UN*: *Seeking cooperation*: *Member countries*: *Cleanup efforts*: *Torrential rains*: Also ask, "what is happening these days in Central Asia?"
II. Understand the basic grammar	Subject = the UN; Verb = to seek; Object = cooperation
III. Clarify the details	Who = the UN What = cooperation (and help with the cleanup) Where = probably at the UN When = shortly after rains in Central Asia Why = Central Asia needs world's help

G) Body and Final Paragraph

1) Body (2nd, 3rd ...paragraphs)

This provides background information, such as the causes of a problem, previous examples, and quotations from experts.

Late-Night Car Crash Injuries Three

Bill Rangtock
November 06, 2006

A Calgary man is in serious condition and two children are recovering from minor injuries after a two-car pileup shortly after midnight on Highway #1 leading west towards Vancouver.

Monty Jones, 18, was returning from work at a hotel complex in Canmore, Alberta around AM this morning when he lost control of his 1996 Camero on a patch of black ice.

The vehicle spun out of control for a short time before broad siding an SUV belonging to the Kendall family of Cochrane.

Neither the driver nor passengers in the SUV received any injuries. However Mr. Jones was taken to hospital with a

fractured rib, and his children were treated for scrapes and bruises.

Constable Fred Smith of the RCMP said that the accident could have been much worse. "The weather was terrible last night, and the visibility was poor. Both parties are lucky to have escaped with their lives," he was quoted as saying.

2) Final paragraph

This part deals with the outcome of the issue and its effects.

Vocabulary

Background:

Previous examples:

Experts:

Issues:

Causes of a problem:

Quotations:

Outcome:

Effects:

Let's take a look at the body and final paragraph of a typical article:

Section	Content	Notes
Headline	**CBD Balcony Collapse Kills Three**	
By-line	*June 20, 2006 – Reuters, Auckland, Philip Germond*	
Lead	Three teenagers were killed Thursday when the balcony of a downtown apartment collapsed during a party.	This tells us the most important points.
Body (2nd paragraph)	Overcrowding of the wood-frame balcony is blamed for the accident, which occurred in an apartment complex built in 1923.	This gives us more details about what happened.
Body (3rd paragraph)	"Ambulances arrived quickly at the scene, but there was nothing the paramedics could do," a police official said.	Even more details here, as well as quotations
Final paragraph	Yesterday, the mayor visited the relatives, and promised a full investigation of the incident.	Results and long-term outlook

Balcony: *Collapse*:

CBD (Central Business District):

Overcrowding: *Wood-frame*:

To blame on: *Accident:*

Apartment complex: *Ambulance*:

Paramedics: *Police official*:

Relatives: *Incident*:

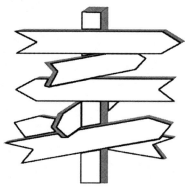

The headline points the way for the rest of the article

Tips IV – Crossword

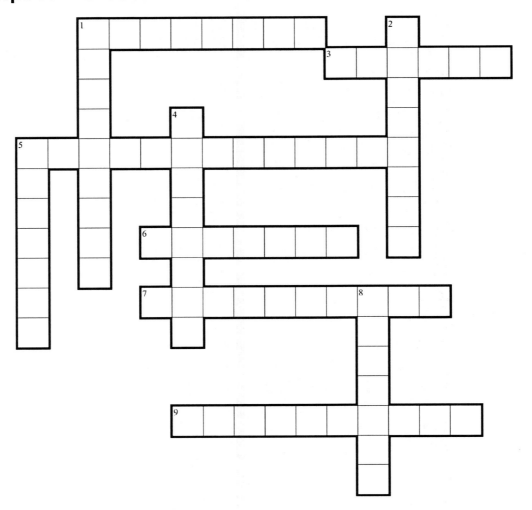

Across

1. The lead is written in order of ___
3. The by-line tells us the news ___
5. The lead is not in ___ order
6. Headlines use a special ___
7. The body provides ___ from experts
9. The body provides ___ information

Down

1. The lead tells us the most ___ information
2. Part of a news article
4. Headline vocabulary is often short and ___
5. Headlines are often about ___ events
8. The final paragraph talks about the ___ of the issues

Section 2: Verbs (Part II)

2.48 To make a comeback

Meaning: To become popular again (trend, person, etc.)

Meaning in your language:

Usage: *A* (person, activity) makes a comeback
1. Disco music is starting <u>to make a comeback</u> in come trendy nightclubs.
Disco music: *Trendy nightclubs:*
2. Elvis Presley songs <u>are making a comeback</u> with today's younger generation.
Younger generation:
3. After so many losses in the boxing ring, I don't think that he <u>will be making a comeback</u>.
Boxing ring:

Related expressions: A new lease on life

                              Second time around

2.49 To make the best of

Meaning: To enjoy something or use something, even though it is not perfect

Meaning in your language:

Usage: *A* (person, group) makes the best of *B* (situation) by doing *C* (action)
1. We <u>made the best of</u> the accommodation even though the hotel room was really cramped.
Accommodation: *Cramped:*
2. Even though the catering for the party was bad, we <u>made the best of it</u> and tried to enjoy ourselves.
Catering: *To enjoy oneself:*
3. The a-bomb survivor <u>made the best of</u> the short speaking time, and made a very moving speech.
A-bomb survivor: *Speaking time:*
Moving speech:

Related expressions: To tough it out

                              To look on the bright side

2.50 To mark a new chapter in

Meaning: Some event is new, good, or very important.

Meaning in your language:

Usage: *A* (event) marks a new chapter in *B* (topic, field of research)

1. The Japanese drug <u>marked a new chapter in</u> the treatment of insomnia.

Insomnia:

2. His novel <u>marked a new chapter in</u> feminist theory.

Novel: *Feminist theory:*

3. The opening of a branch office in Tokyo <u>marks a new chapter in</u> the history of this American company.

Branch office:

Related expressions: A turning point

                                   A milestone

2.51 To mark the first time that)

Meaning: Something special happens for the first time.

Meaning in your language:

Usage: *A* (situation, event) marks the first time that *B* (something special or unusual)

1. The decision by the court <u>marked the first time that</u> smokers were awarded damages.

Decision by the court: *Smokers:*

Awarded damages:

2. John Glenn's short spaceflight <u>marked the first time</u> in history <u>that</u> an American ventured into space.

Spaceflight:

To venture into something:

3. The inaugural ceremony <u>marked the first time that</u> a woman was elected mayor in that city.

Inaugural ceremony: *Elected:*

Related expressions: A milestone

                                   Groundbreaking

2.52 To mean (that)

Meaning: One fact implies another fact.

Meaning in your language:

Usage: *A* (some fact) means that *B* (related fact)

1. The strong performance by this blue chip company <u>means that</u> its stock will probably rise this year.

Performance: *Blue chip company:*

2. This continued cold weather <u>means</u> trouble for the farmers in this isolated community.

Continued cold weather: *Isolated:*

3. The decrease in the number of travelers <u>means</u> tough times ahead for the airline industry.

Travelers: *Tough times:*   *Airline industry:*

Related expressions: In other words

                                               To make a long story short

 **Famous Saying**

Action is eloquence.
(Shakespeare, 1564-1616)

2.53 To open a window (on / into)

Meaning: To show or introduce something, usually secret or unseen

Meaning in your language:

Usage: *A* (person, event) opens a window on *B* (person, group, event, activity)

1. The entrance of the United Nations peacekeepers into the small country <u>has opened a window on</u> their mysterious culture.

United Nations peacekeepers: *Culture:*

2. Reality television shows <u>open a window into</u> peoples' private lives by broadcasting their behavior 24 hours a day.

Reality television shows: *Private lives:*

To broadcast:

3. The fall of the Communist government in the late 1980's <u>opened a window on</u> everyday life in the Soviet Union.

Communist government: *Everyday life:*

Soviet Union:

Related expressions: To peer into

          To catch a glimpse of

Television opens a window on other cultures

2.54 To open its doors to

Meaning: To welcome someone; to be friendly towards someone; to offer help

Meaning in your language:

Usage: *A* (group) opens its doors to *B* (person, group)

1. The nation decided <u>to open its doors to</u> the boat people from the impoverished island.

The nation: *Boat people:*

Impoverished island:

2. The conservative golf club is finally <u>opening its doors to</u> minorities.

Conservative: *Golf club:*   *Minorities:*

3. The church decided <u>to open its doors to</u> the homeless by providing a shelter.

Homeless: *Shelter:*

Related expressions: To roll out the red carpet

                                     An open-door policy

2.55 To plead guilty

Meaning: To admit to a judge that you committed a crime (courtroom vocabulary)

Meaning in your language:

Usage: *A* (person) pleads guilty to *B* (crime)

1. He <u>pleaded guilty</u> to the manslaughter charge and was sentenced to 18 months in prison.

Manslaughter charge: *Prison:*

2. If he <u>pleads guilty</u> he may be sent to jail.

To send to jail:

3. He <u>pleaded not guilty</u> and said that he was framed by the police.

To plead "Not guilty":   *Framed by the police:*

Related expressions: To take your lumps

                                     To take the blame

2.56 To pour a lot of money into

Meaning: To spend a lot of money on something (over time)
Meaning in your language:

Usage: *A* (person, group) pours a lot of money into *B* (project)

1. He's <u>poured a lot of money into</u> that sports car. It seems to need repairs almost every other week.

Sports car: *Every other week:*

2. The fledgling company did well by <u>pouring a lot of money into</u> research and development.

Fledgling company: *Research and development:*

3. <u>Money poured into</u> the telethon after the little girl with leukemia gave her speech.

Telethon: *Leukemia:*

Related expressions: A money pit
                                To throw money at

2.57 To press charges

Meaning: To take someone to court
Meaning in your language:

Usage: *A* (person, group) presses charges against *B* (person, group)

1. The federal government <u>is pressing charges</u> because the accused traveled across state lines from New York to New Jersey.

The federal government: *The accused:*

State lines:

2. The restaurant manager said that he wouldn't <u>press charges</u> if the customer paid for the broken dishes.

Restaurant manager: *Broken dishes:*

3. I don't want <u>to press charges</u>, but he shouldn't have borrowed my car without asking.

To borrow: *Without asking:*

Related expressions: To throw the book at
                                To accuse

2.58 To pull out of

Meaning: To retreat; to leave an area

Meaning in your language:

Usage: *A* (person group) pulls out of *B* (country or region)

1. Tanks are finally <u>pulling out of</u> the war-torn area now that the cease-fire has been signed.

Tanks: *War-torn:*   *Cease-fire:*

2. The demonstrators want their government <u>to pull out of</u> the negotiations regarding the Taiwanese issue.

Demonstrators: *Negotiations:*

Taiwanese issue:

3. Many people were surprised when America <u>pulled out of</u> the Kyoto Accord on global warming.

Kyoto Accord: *Global warming (see 1.22):*

Related expressions: To scale back

                                      To drop out of

2.59 To put in / to put … into

Meaning: To work hard; to do your best

Meaning in your language:

Usage: *A* (person) puts in a lot of *B* (time, energy, effort) for *C* (goal).

1. I <u>put in</u> the hours at work, but I never seem to get promoted.

To get promoted:

2. If you'd <u>put</u> more effort <u>into</u> your studies, you could increase your grade point average.

More effort: *Grade point average:*

3. The judges quickly realized that the ice skaters had <u>put</u> a lot of thought <u>into</u> their routine.

Ice skaters: *Routine:*

Related expressions: To brush up on

                                      To work like a dog

2.60 To put on the market

Meaning: To begin selling something

Meaning in your language:

Usage: *A* (person, company) puts *B* (product) on the market

1. The pharmaceutical company has no idea when the new product will be <u>put on the market</u> in Japan.

Pharmaceutical company: *New product:*

2. She expects that the music label will <u>put</u> her debut CD <u>on the market</u> sometime next autumn.

Music label: *Debut CD:*

3. The toy was <u>put on the market</u> in January, but recalled in May because of consumer complaints.

Recalled: *Consumer complaints:*

Related expressions: To be out

To hit the shelves

2.61 To release

Meaning #1: To make something public

Meaning in your language:

Usage: *A* (person, group) releases *B* (information, product)

1. The motion picture will <u>be released</u> across the country in about 6 weeks.

Motion picture: *Across the country:*

2. The manager says that <u>he is not going to release</u> the report on quality control because it contains company secrets.

Quality control: *Company secrets:*

Meaning #2: To let someone go free, to let someone out of prison

Meaning in your language:

1. The United Nations has requested that the political prisoner <u>be released</u> immediately.

United Nations: *Political prisoner:*

2. The bank robber said that he <u>would release</u> the hostages for money.

Bank robber: *Hostages:*

Related expressions: To make a splash (Meaning #1)

To unhand (Meaning #2)

2.62 To remain to be seen

Meaning: To be unclear or uncertain

Meaning in your language:

Usage: It remains to be seen whether **A** (possible future event)

1. Whether the conglomerate can survive in this difficult economy <u>remains to be seen</u>.

Conglomerate: *To survive:*

Difficult economy:

2. It <u>remains to be seen</u> whether her second album will be as creative as her debut single last year.

Second album: *Debut single:*

3. It <u>remains to be seen</u> whether the trucking company can recover the revenue they lost after the mishap last year.

Trucking company: *To recover revenue:*

Mishap:

Related expression: To be anybody's guess

A matter for speculation

Tomorrow's weather remains to be seen

104

2.63 To remain upbeat (about)

Meaning: To feel positive or optimistic, even though something is difficult

Meaning in your language:

Usage: *A* (person) remains upbeat about *B* (possibility) despite/even though *C* (some difficulty).

1. The prime minister told the newspaper that he <u>remains upbeat</u> despite the threat of impeachment.

Prime minister: *Impeachment:*

2. She <u>remained upbeat</u> even during the difficult chemotherapy treatment.

Chemotherapy treatment:

3. The FBI <u>remains upbeat about</u> catching the culprit, even though there are few clues in the case.

Culprit: *Clues:*   *Case:*

Related expressions: Undaunted by

Eternally optimistic

2.64 To ruffle some feathers

Meaning: To offend someone, or make someone angry

Meaning in your language:

Usage: *A* (person) ruffles some feathers by *B* (action)

1. The rock star's rudeness during the television interview really <u>ruffled some feathers</u>.

Rock star: *Rudeness:*

Television interview:

2. The goodwill ambassador <u>ruffled some feathers</u> by suggesting that his job could only be done by a man, not a woman.

Goodwill ambassador:

3. The suggestion to use the vacant land for a paint factory <u>ruffled the feathers</u> of nearby residents.

Vacant land: *Paint factory:*

Nearby residents:

Related expressions: To fan the flames

To get someone's goat

2.65 To rule out

Meaning: To decide against; to refuse something

Meaning in your language:

Usage: *A* (person, group) rules out *B* (action) because *C* (reason).

1. The commander <u>ruled out</u> military action against the group because of the mountainous terrain.

Commander: *Military action:*

Mountainous terrain:

2. The health minister <u>ruled out</u> widespread vaccinations against the disease because it was unnecessary this year.

Health minister: *Widespread vaccinations:*

Unnecessary:

3. The munitions factory <u>ruled out</u> heightened security as too expensive.

Munitions factory: *To heighten security:*

Related expressions: To dismiss something

                                       To veto

2.66 To run into

Meaning #1: To accidentally meet

Meaning in your language:

Usage: *A* (person) runs into *B* (person) at/on *C* (place)

1. You'll never guess who I <u>ran into</u> at the quay - my old teacher from junior high school!

Quay: *Junior high school:*

2. It was a surprise <u>running into</u> you at the concert last night. I didn't know you liked classical music.

Meaning #2: To have some problems or difficulties

Meaning in your language:

1. The importer <u>ran into</u> difficulties with the Chamber of Commerce.

Importer: *Chamber of Commerce:*

2. He <u>ran into</u> problems with his girlfriend, and they finally broke up.

To break up:

Related expressions: To bump into (Meaning #1)

                                       To face (Meaning #2) (See 2.25)

2.67 To seek to

Meaning: To wish to do something, plan to do something, or try to do something

Meaning in your language:

Usage: *A* (person, group) seeks to *B* (plan)

1. The chairperson <u>is seeking to</u> resign after this term expires.

Chairperson: *To resign:*   *Term expires:*

2. The grassroots protesters <u>are seeking to</u> block government use of the farmland.

Grassroots protestors: *To block something:*

Farmland:

3. As an author, he <u>is seeking to</u> blend his African-American heritage with his view of contemporary life.

To blend: *Heritage:*   *Contemporary life:*

Related expressions: Iron in the fire

To set one's sights on

2.68 To see the light at the end of the tunnel

Meaning: To near the end of a long period of difficulties

Meaning in your language:

Usage: After *A* (bad condition, situation), *B* (person, group) can see the light at the end of the tunnel

1. After four years of hard study, the beleaguered graduate student <u>could</u> finally <u>see the light at the end of the tunnel</u>.

Beleaguered: *Graduate student:*

2. Building the expressway was difficult, but the workers <u>could</u> finally <u>see the light at the end of the tunnel</u>.

Expressway:

3. If I could <u>see the light at the end of the tunnel</u>, then I would do my best…

To do one's best:

Related expressions: To break free

To make it through

107

2.69 To shape up to be

Meaning #1: To become

Meaning in your language:

Usage: **A** (situation, person) shapes up to be **B** (description)

1. He <u>is</u> really <u>shaping up to be</u> a great employee, in terms of his diligence and enthusiasm.

Diligence: *Enthusiasm:*

2. This <u>is shaping up to be</u> an exciting hockey season because of the skill of the goalie.

Hockey season: *Goalie:*

Meaning #2: <Shape up or ship out>: Someone tells you to do better work

Meaning in your language:

1. My boss told me <u>to shape up or ship out</u>, so I've decided to look for a new job.

2. The assistant manager of that menswear department had better <u>shape up or ship out</u>, in my opinion.

Assistant manager: *Menswear department:*

Related expressions: Turning out to be (Meaning #1)

                                     To get one's act together (Meaning #2)

2.70 To shoulder

Meaning: To accept responsibility for something

Meaning in your language:

Usage: **A** (person, organization) shoulders **B** (job, duty, responsibility)

1. His parents <u>shouldered</u> the financial burden for his college fees. He didn't have to work at all!

Financial burden: *College fees:*

2. She admitted that she had been drinking, and said she would <u>shoulder</u> the responsibility for the fine.

Responsibility: *(Traffic) fine:*

3. I <u>shouldered</u> the burden of telling the family the bad news.

The bad news:

Related expression: A cross to bear

                               To carry

2.71 To show promise

Meaning: People are hopeful about something that could be good or useful.

Meaning in your language:

Usage: **A** (person, product, plan) shows promise for **B** (purpose, goal, role)

1. Aspirin <u>is showing promise</u> as a treatment for heart disease.

Aspirin:　　　　*As a (see 1.1):*　　　　*Heart disease:*

2. The rookie <u>shows promise</u>, but he needs to work harder.

Rookie:

3. That medical student <u>shows promise</u> and his endeavors should be encouraged.

Medical student:　　　　*Endeavors:*　　　　*To encourage:*

Related expressions:　　　　Light at the end of the tunnel (See 2.68)

　　　　　　　　　　　　　　To pin one's hopes on

She really shows promise as a cheerleader

2.72 To sink in

Meaning: Someone finally understands or feels something.

Meaning in your language:

Usage: *A* (situation, fact) sinks in

1. The extent of the damage only <u>sunk in</u> when I saw the pictures from Ground Zero.

Extent of the damage: *Ground Zero:*

2. It didn't <u>sink in</u> that I had won the medal until I finally stood on the podium and received it.

To win a medal: *Podium:*

3. When will it <u>sink in</u> that you don't have any money left in the bank!!

Money left in the bank:

Related Expressions: The other shoe has dropped

                                                     To dawn on (See 2.18)

2.73 To snap up

Meaning: To quickly accept an offer; to buy something eagerly.

Meaning in your language:

Usage: *A* (person, group) snaps up *B* (offer, object)

1. The generous job offer by the talent scout <u>was</u> quickly <u>snapped up</u> by the university student.

Generous: *Job offer:*   *Talent scout:*

2. Collectors <u>snapped up</u> his new CD and they are now sold out at most stores.

Collectors: *Sold out:*

3. Souvenirs of the soccer game <u>were snapped up</u> by ardent fans as soon as they went on sale.

Souvenirs: *Ardent fans:*

Related expressions: Selling like hotcakes

                                                     A feeding frenzy

2.74 To spur … into (action)

Meaning: To force someone to do something; to make something happen
Meaning in your language:

Usage: **A** (person, group) spurs **B** (person, group) into action
Passive tense: A (person, group) is spurred into action by B (person, group, situation)

1. The police <u>were spurred into</u> action against the youth gangs after the altercation at the festival.

Youth gangs: *Altercation:*

2. He <u>was spurred into</u> action and became a peace activist after his visit to Hiroshima.

Peace activist:

3. The media attention <u>will spur</u> small businesses <u>into</u> protesting the new tax.

Media attention: *To protest:*

Related expressions: To goad
                                 To light a fire under

2.75 To stand by

Meaning #1: To support; to agree with; to offer help
Meaning in your language:

Usage: **A** (person, group) stands by **B** (person, group, decision, action)

1. The movie studio <u>stood by</u> its decision to release the controversial movie.

Movie studio: *To release a movie*:

Controversial:

2. She <u>stood by</u> her husband even after she saw him kissing another woman.

Meaning #2: To do nothing / to wait, even though it is difficult
Meaning in your language:

1. I can't <u>stand by</u> and let you make such a stupid decision!

2. The police officer started CPR on the man having the heart attack, instead of just <u>standing by</u> and waiting for the ambulance.

CPR (cardiopulmonary resuscitation):

Heart attack: *Ambulance:*

Related expressions: Through thick and thin (Meaning #1)
                                 To wait on the sidelines (Meaning #2)

2.76 To stave off

Meaning: To prevent something bad from happening

Meaning in your language:

Usage: *A* (person, company) staves off *B* (something bad) by *C* (action)

1. The winery was able <u>to stave off</u> foreclosure by getting money from the local savings and loan.

Winery: *Foreclosure:*   *Savings and loan:*

2. The company <u>staved off</u> a general strike by giving the workers a raise.

General strike: *A raise:*

3. The artist is hoping <u>to stave off</u> the closure of the gallery by asking the government for financial help.

Closure: *Gallery:*   *Financial help:*

Related expressions: To bite the bullet

To tighten our belts

2.77 To step in

Meaning: To take action; to volunteer

Meaning in your language:

Usage: *A* (person, group) steps in to *B* (some action)

1. The victim was attacked when he <u>stepped in</u> to stop the barroom brawl.

Victim: *Barroom brawl:*

2. I don't want <u>to step in</u>. I want her to figure out a solution without my help.

To figure out:

3. The understudy <u>stepped in</u> and played the role when the lead caught the flu.

Understudy: *The lead:*   *Flu (influenza):*

Related expressions: To enter the fray

To fill a vacancy

2.78 To stir up controversy

Meaning: To encourage debate; to make people think

Meaning in your language:

Usage: *A* (person, group, topic) stirs up controversy

1. The new movie is going <u>to stir up controversy</u> regarding the treatment of minorities in society.

The treatment of: *Minorities:*

2. That comedian loves <u>to stir up controversy</u> whenever she gets a chance.

Comedian: *To get a chance:*

3. <u>Stirring up controversy</u> about overpopulation is easier than finding a solution.

Overpopulation:

Related expressions: To spark a debate

To cause a stir (See 2.10)

 **Famous Saying**

The unexamined life is <u>not worth</u> living. (See 3.44)

(Socrates 470-399 BC)

2.79 To take a breather (from)

Meaning: To rest; to take a vacation from something

Meaning in your language:

Usage: **A** (person) takes a breather from **B** (situation, person, activity)

1. The heiress said that she plans <u>to take a breather from</u> her hard schedule and spend two weeks in Monaco.

Heiress: *Monaco:*

2. I'd like <u>to take a breather</u> but it's difficult in the current economic situation.

Economic situation:

3. The shot putter <u>took a breather</u> last week and visited his hometown.

Shot putter: *Hometown:*

Related expressions: To chill out

                                To take a break

They're taking a breather at the beach

2.80 To take aim at

Meaning: To argue against something; to fight or attack

Meaning in your language:

Usage: *A* (person, group) take aim at *B* (person, group, situation)

1. The church group <u>was taking aim at</u> stores in the neighborhood that sell alcohol to teenagers.

Church group: *Alcohol:*   *Teenagers:*

2. Parliament is debating a new law that <u>takes aim at</u> people who drink and drive.

Parliament: Debating: *Drinking and driving:*

3. The boarder police <u>took aim at</u> smugglers by using specially-trained sniffer dogs.

Smugglers: *Specially-trained:*

Sniffer dogs:

Related expressions: To take on

                                           To take offence at

2.81 To take a toll on

Meaning: To cause trouble; to cost someone time, money or effort

Meaning in your language:

Usage: *A* (bad situation) takes a toll on *B* (person, group, resource)

1. The long court battle <u>is taking a toll on</u> his health.

Court battle: *Someone's health:*

2. The concern over Mad Cow Disease <u>is taking a toll on</u> the dairy industry.

Mad Cow Disease: *Dairy industry:*

3. Wheat prices are rising as the drought <u>takes its toll on</u> this year's crops.

Wheat prices: *Drought:*   *Crops:*

Related expressions: To wear him/her down

                                           To take the wind out of one's sails

2.82 To take a turn for the better / the worse

Meaning: To change direction; to get better/worse

Meaning in your language:

Usage: *A* (condition) takes a turn for the *B* (worse/better)

1. The condition of the patient appeared to be good, but he <u>took a turn for the worse</u> and then died this morning.

Condition of the patient:

2. If the stock market doesn't <u>take a turn for the better</u> soon, I'm going to lose all my money.

Stock market:

3. The ballet dancer's career <u>took a turn for the better</u> after her successful tour of Europe.

Ballet dancer: *To tour Europe:*

Related expressions: A downturn/ an upturn

To make a turnaround

2.83 (Not) to take… lying down

Meaning: To refuse to quit; to keep trying; to counterattack

Meaning in your language:

Usage: *A* (person, group) takes/doesn't take *B* (some news) lying down.

1. The workers decided <u>not to take</u> the layoffs <u>lying down</u>. They formed a union and are now fighting for justice.

Layoffs: *A union:*   *Justice:*

2. That brilliant doctor <u>isn't taking</u> news of the outbreak <u>lying down</u>. She's already working on a vaccine.

Outbreak: *Vaccine:*

3. He refused <u>to take</u> the news of the cancer <u>lying down</u>. He and his doctors are aggressively fighting the disease.

Cancer: *To fight aggressively:*

Related expressions: To get one's second wind

To get back on one's feet

2.84 To take one's case to / up with

Meaning: To meet with someone to explain your beliefs or argue your position

Meaning in your language:

Usage: **A** (person, group) takes their case to **B** (group, place)

1. He is unhappy with the decision of the lower courts, and says that he <u>will take</u> his <u>case</u> all the way <u>to</u> the Supreme Court if necessary.

Lower court: *Supreme Court:*

2. You can <u>take</u> your <u>case up with</u> the chair of the board, but I don't think you will have any success.

Chair of the board:

3. The neighborhood committee wanted to stop the new construction project, so they <u>took</u> their <u>case to</u> the municipal authorities.

Neighborhood committee: *Municipal authorities:*
Construction project:

Related expressions: To have a word with
                                  To bend someone's ear

2.85 To take / treat .... seriously

Meaning: To pay attention to something; to be nervous about something

Meaning in your language:

Usage: **A** (person, group) takes **B** (news) seriously

1. The airport officials <u>took</u> the bomb threat <u>seriously</u> and closed the departures lounge.

Airport officials: *Bomb threat:*
Departures lounge:

2. Nobody <u>took</u> the reports of his alcoholism <u>seriously</u> until he had the car accident.

Alcoholism: *Car accident:*

3. Despite his batting average, the fans never <u>take</u> him <u>seriously</u>.

Batting average: *Fans:*

Related expressions: To prick up one's ears
                                  To get one's attention

2.86 To take the mickey out of

Meaning: To make fun of someone; to tease someone (impolite)

Meaning in your language:

Usage: *A* (person) takes the mickey out of *B* (person, group) for *C* (reason).

1. His father <u>took the mickey out of</u> him for dropping out of school.

To drop out of school:

2. My boss really <u>took the mickey out of</u> me for losing those files.

To lose files:

3. Don't <u>take the mickey out of</u> me! It's not my fault that I lost the car keys!

Not one's fault:

Related expressions: To grill

          To blame

2.87 To take the stance (that)

Meaning: To decide on something, argue for something, or fight for something

Meaning in your language:

Usage: *A* (person or group) takes the stance that *B* (argument)

1. The senator wanted to read the report, but the army <u>took the stance that</u> it should remain classified.

To remain classified:

2. Although the train lost his luggage, they <u>took the stance that</u> it was his fault for not tagging it properly.

Luggage: *His fault:*   *To tag luggage:*

3. If you <u>are going to take</u> that <u>stance</u>, then there is no way for us to reach a compromise.

Reach a compromise:

Related expressions: To adopt a position

          To dig one's heels in

2.88 To teach someone (a lesson)

Meaning #1: To punish someone for doing something bad

Meaning in your language:

Usage: *A* (person, group) teaches *B* (person, group) a lesson by *C* (punishment)

1. The company decided <u>to teach</u> the lazy workers <u>a lesson</u> by charging them a penalty for arriving late.

Lazy: *To charge a penalty:*

To arrive late:

2. She hoped <u>to teach</u> the waiter <u>a lesson</u> by not tipping him for his poor service.

Waiter: *To tip:*   *Poor service:*

Meaning #2: Someone is giving advice or criticism

Meaning in your language:

1. You have a hangover this morning? That <u>will teach</u> you <u>not to</u> drink heavily the night before an examination.

Hangover: *To drink heavily:*

2. A: Maybe cutting off your allowance <u>will teach</u> you <u>to do</u> your chores on time!
   B: But dad...I need that money!

To cut off an allowance: *Chores:*

Related expressions: To get back at someone (Meaning #1)

To take one's lumps (Meaning #2)

I hope this teaches him a lesson!

2.89 To tighten one's belt

Meaning: To conserve money, or reduce spending

Meaning in your language:

Usage: *A* (person, group) tightens his/her belt

1. The company president asked the board of directors <u>to tighten their belts</u> and to accept a pay cut.

President: *Board of directors:*   *Pay cut:*

2. If these <u>belt-tightening</u> measures don't work, we may be forced to close our business.

Measures: *Forced to close:*

3. Let's <u>tighten our belts</u> by only eating dinner at home.

To eat at home:

Related expressions: To tighten the purse-strings

To cut back

2.90 To touch base with

Meaning: To make contact with or communicate with someone

Meaning in your language:

Usage: *A* (person, group) touches base with *B* (person, group)

1. Even after he became very successful, he still liked <u>to touch base with</u> his friends in the old neighborhood.

To become successful:

2. The singer/songwriter <u>touches base with</u> her agent at least once a week.

Singer/songwriter: *Agent:*

3. Please excuse me - I have <u>to touch base with</u> the home office.

Home office:

Related expressions: To drop someone a line

Don't be a stranger

2.91 To trade barbs

Meaning: Two people are arguing, criticizing or debating.

Meaning in your language:

Usage: **A** (person, group) and **B** (another person, group) trade barbs over **C** (some issue)

1. The mayoral candidates <u>traded barbs</u> on the issue of overspending in government.

Mayoral candidates: *Overspending:*

2. Instead of <u>trading barbs</u>, let's negotiate properly and try to find a solution.

To negotiate: *To find a solution:*

3. The bank teller was fired for <u>trading barbs</u> with his customer.

Bank teller:

Related expressions: Sniping

A volley of criticism

2.92 To turn over a new leaf

Meaning: To reform, start fresh, or start again

Meaning in your language:

Usage: **A** (person, group) turns over a new leaf

1. The disgraced police chief said that he <u>had turned over a new leaf</u>, and asked the review board for his old job back.

Disgraced: *Police chief:*   *Review board:*

2. If you want <u>to turn over a new leaf</u>, you shouldn't associate with such a bad lot after school.

To associate with someone: *A bad lot:*

3. The actress said that the drug rehabilitation program had helped her <u>to turn over a new leaf</u>.

Drug rehabilitation program:

Related expressions: Water under the bridge

A leopard can't change his stripes

2.93 To walk on eggshells

Meaning: To be very careful; to try not to offend someone

Meaning in your language:

Usage: *A* (person, group) walks on eggshells after *B* (mistake, bad behavior)

1. The leader of the opposition <u>is walking on eggshells</u> after her unkind words were printed in all the major newspapers.

Leader of the opposition:

2. That clothing store <u>is walking on eggshells</u> after the complaint from the consumer rights group.

Clothing store: *Consumer rights group:*

3. The export supplier <u>was walking on eggshells</u> following the report of more cattle disease in the country.

Export supplier: *Cattle disease:*

Related expressions: To tread softly
                                  To hold back

2.94 To wash .... hands of

Meaning: To end a relationship

Meaning in your language:

Usage: *A* (person, group) washes their hands of *B* (a person, group, situation)

1. He <u>washed his hands of</u> his fiancée after she started dating someone else.

Fiancée: *To date:*

2. The company <u>washed its hands of</u> the supplier when the goods were not delivered on time.

Supplier: *Not delivered on time:*

3. The station <u>washed its hands of</u> the news anchor after his incarceration.

News anchor: *Incarceration:*

Related expressions: To have nothing to do with
                                  To sever all ties with

Mini-Quiz: Verbs Part II

Part A

1.You can't just ..... let your son make such a big mistake.
a) make a comeback   **b)** rule out   **c)** run into   **d)** stand by and

2.It is too early ..... another price increase later in the season.
a) to step in   **b)** open its doors to   **c)** to sink in   **d)** to rule out

3.The department store says that they plan .... if anyone is caught stealing goods.
a) to stir up controversy   **b)** to put in   **c)** to press charges   **d)** remain upbeat

4.The new wonder drug ..... as a treatment for cancer.
a) remains upbeat   **b)** marks new chapters   **c)** shows promise   **d)** shoulders

5.The committee ... their report early next week.
a) will release **b)** will take it lying down **c)** will open a window **d)** will take aim

6.The criminal ... in order to avoid a long trial.
a) pleaded guilty   **b)** snapped up   **c)** remained to be seen   **d)** ruffled some feathers

7.The supermarket says that they are .... open a new store downtown next year.
a) aiming at   **b)** are opening its doors to   **c)** seeking to   **d)** releasing

8.The embarrassed mayor seems to be … after the recent bribery scandal.

a) sinking in   **b)** trading barbs   **c)** snapping up   **d)** walking on eggshells

9.The 18-hour shifts at the hospital are … on the health of the young doctors.

a) shaping up   **b)** taking a toll   **c)** making a comeback   **d)** remaining upbeat

10. Middle managers must …. so that companies will survive in this poor economy.

a) tighten their belts   **b)** trade barbs   **c)** stir up controversy   **d)** take a breather

11. The low pressure system over the city … this bad weather will continue for the next few days.

a) means that   **b)** pulls out of   **c)** rules out   **d)** shows promise

12. Sanchez told reporters that he wants to … the race because of his leg injury.

a) step in   **b)** snap up   **c)** pull out of   **d)** shoulder

13. He hopes he doesn't … any of his ex-wives at the party.

a) touch base with   **b)** take aim at   **c)** pull out of   **d)** run into

14. This is really … to be a great week for you.

a) putting on the market   **b)** ruling out   **c)** shaping up   **d)** showing promise

15. The private sector will have to … the responsibility for the mistake.

a) stave off   **b)** shoulder   **c)** trade barbs   **d)** step in

Part B

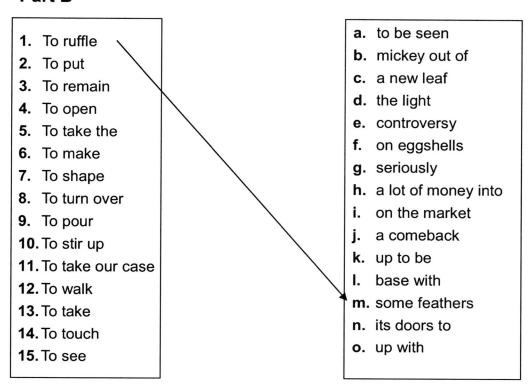

1. To ruffle
2. To put
3. To remain
4. To open
5. To take the
6. To make
7. To shape
8. To turn over
9. To pour
10. To stir up
11. To take our case
12. To walk
13. To take
14. To touch
15. To see

a. to be seen
b. mickey out of
c. a new leaf
d. the light
e. controversy
f. on eggshells
g. seriously
h. a lot of money into
i. on the market
j. a comeback
k. up to be
l. base with
m. some feathers
n. its doors to
o. up with

Part C

E.g. may / that / as / be / it : <u>Be that as it may</u>

1. comeback / to / a / make   :_____
2. best / of / to / the / make   :_____
3. to / chapter / a / new / mark / in   :_____
4. that / time / first / to / the / mark   :_____
5. to / a / on / window / open   :_____
6. its / doors / to / open / to   :_____
7. pour / lot / money / into / of / a / to   :_____
8. out / of / to / pull   :_____
9. market / on / the / put / to   :_____
10. remain / be / to / to / seen   :_____

125

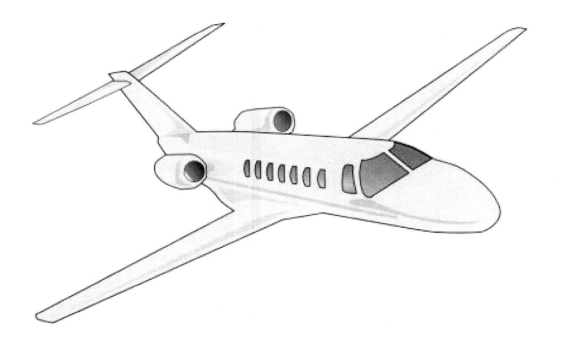

Too much air travel can take a toll on your health (see 2.81)

TIPS V: Business and Finance Websites

These are some of the best places online to read about business and finance:

News Agency	Website	Notes
Asia Times	www.atimes.com	Information on China, Japan, Korea, the whole of Southeast Asia, and the world.
Bloomberg	www.bloomberg.com	Investment news, market data, and multimedia (tv, radio, podcasts)
Clearstation	www.clearstation.com	Coverage of sectors and industries; best and worst stocks
CNN	money.cnn.com	Stocks, plus business and technology, jobs, and the economy
eFinancial News	www.efinancialnews.com	Special features about European investments

Multimedia: *Sectors*:   *Industries*:

Features:

Business and Finance Websites Cont.

News Agency	Website	Notes
Financial Times	www.ft.com	London-based financial news
Forbes	www.forbes.com	Covering business and technology, stock market, entrepreneurs, and personal finance
Investors.com	www.investors.com	News, research, and help with how to invest
Market Watch	www.marketwatch.com	Personal investing tools and research
Morningstar	www.morningstar.com	Many tools for analyzing stocks and funds
MSN Network	Moneycentral.msn.com	Excellent ratings system for stocks
Reuters	www.reuters.com	Corporate profiles, plus information on stocks, funds, options, bonds…
Yahoo! Finance	finance.yahoo.com	Help with portfolio selection

Stocks: *Funds:*   *Options:*

Bonds:

 **Famous Saying**

Bad news travels fast.

(Anonymous)

TIPS VI: Business and Financial Content

A) <u>Website Structure</u>

Most business and finance websites offer many different kinds of information.

Dow Up 100 Points on Good Housing News

1) News articles
(the state of the stock market etc.)

Mutual Funds Best for Long-Term Income

Will Bear Market Continue Next Year?

Click here for today's market recap

2) Advice columns
(how to invest, where to invest, etc.)

4) Other information (currency exchange rates, stock market overviews, bonds and debentures, options, stock valuations)

3) Financial predictions
(future interest rates, stock market trends, etc.)

B) The Stock Market

1) Articles on the stock market use very special vocabulary.

Here is a list of some of some key words for describing a stock chart:

English	Your Language
1 yr (year) target	
Change (from yesterday)	
Div. (Dividend) yield	
EPS (Earnings per share)	
Industry	
Last trade	
Market cap (capitalization)	
P/E (Price-to-earnings ratio)	
Prev. (previous) close	
ROI (Return On Investment)	
Sector	
Ticker (Symbol)	
Volume	

2) There is also special vocabulary for describing the shape of a stock chart.

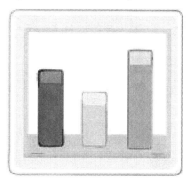

These words tell you how the price of a stock is changing:

English	Your Language	Direction of Price Change
A crash		⬇ DOWN (strongly)
A dip		⬇ DOWN
A price breakout		⬆ UP (strongly)
Bearish		⬇ DOWN (long-term)
Bullish		⬆ UP (long-term)
To bottom out		⬏ DOWN, then STEADY or UP

Stock Prices Cont.

English	Your Language	Direction of Price Change
To climb steadily		↑ UP (long-term)
To drop steadily		↓ DOWN (long-term)
To peak / to top out		↰ UP, then STEADY or DOWN
To plummet		↓ DOWN (strongly)
To remain flat		→ NO CHANGE
To soar		↑ UP (Strongly)

2.1) Let's use the vocabulary above in some real-world sentences.

1. Gold prices <u>soared</u> today on fears of North Korean missile tests.
Gold prices: *On fears of*:   *Missile tests*:

2. Shares of the stock <u>plummeted</u> when the insider trading became public.
Stock shares: *Insider trading*:

3.The Nikkei index is <u>bearish</u> this year but the NASDAQ market remains bullish.
Nikkei index: *NASDAQ*:

4. Stocks for the pharmaceutical company <u>remain flat</u> despite a banner year for sales.

Pharmaceutical company: *Banner year*:

5. Shares in the dot-com company are <u>climbing steadily</u> following the IPO last week.

Dot-com company: *IPO(Initial Public Offering)*:

6. It looks like this year's bear market has finally <u>bottomed out</u>.
Bear market:

7. My favorite small-cap stock <u>dipped</u> after the recent merger.
Small-cap stock: *Merger*:

My portfolio has soared recently

C) <u>Financial News Articles</u>

Financial news articles have almost the same structure as general news articles.

Most financial news articles are built from the following elements:

1) Headline

2) By-line

3) Lead (1st sentence or paragraph)

This usually gives you the most important information (5 W's).

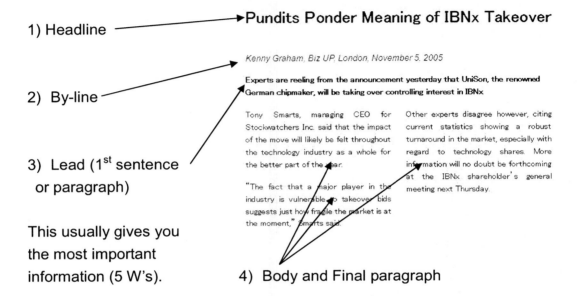

Pundits Ponder Meaning of IBNx Takeover

Kenny Graham, Biz UP, London, November 5, 2005

Experts are reeling from the announcement yesterday that UniSon, the renowned German chipmaker, will be taking over controlling interest in IBNx.

Tony Smarts, managing CEO for Stockwatchers Inc. said that the impact of the move will likely be felt throughout the technology industry as a whole for the better part of the year.

"The fact that a major player in the industry is vulnerable to takeover bids suggests just how fragile the market is at the moment," Smarts said.

Other experts disagree however, citing current statistics showing a robust turnaround in the market, especially with regard to technology shares. More information will no doubt be forthcoming at the IBNx shareholder's general meeting next Thursday.

4) Body and Final paragraph

The body gives you more information about the topic, and sometimes quotations. The article can end with more background to the story, or the results/outcome, or even with the long-term outlook.

Let's take a detailed look at a typical financial news article:

Section	Content	Notes
Headline	**IBN Buys NovaSoft Chip Factory**	
By-line	*April 16, 2006 – Bizjournals, NY, Harvey Norm*	
Lead	Novasoft, a IC-manufacturing company in New Jersey, is selling its largest factory to IBN, a spokesperson announced Wednesday.	Most important information: *What* = Sale of factory *Where* = NJ *Who* = Novasoft and IBN *When* = Near future
Body (paragraph 2)	IBN will use the new plant to aid production of its 5th-generation wireless network.	Details about the market
Body (paragraph 3)	"No layoffs are expected at the plant," said foreman Rob Reiter. He did not mention if salaries would remain the same.	Even more details, plus quotations
Final paragraph	Some analysts had predicted that the sale was a means of increasing income to cover short-term loans. While the sale has been finalized, it may take 6 months for the transition to be complete.	Background, results and long-term outlook

Chip:

Manufacturing:

To aid:

Foreman:

Analyst:

To finalize:

IC (Integrated circuit):

Spokesperson:

Wireless network:

Salary:

Short-term loans:

Transition:

D) <u>Financial Advice</u>

Financial advisors write columns giving us their opinion about how to invest. Financial advisor.

The structure of this kind of article is a little bit different:

1) Headline

The headline gives us the writer's viewpoint.

2) By-line

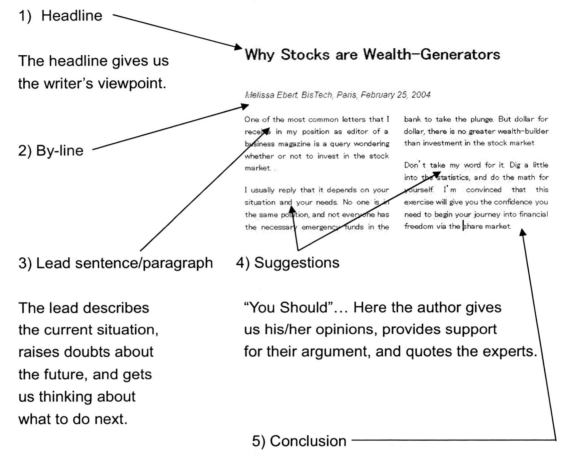

Why Stocks are Wealth-Generators

Melissa Ebert, BisTech, Paris, February 25, 2004

One of the most common letters that I receive in my position as editor of a business magazine is a query wondering whether or not to invest in the stock market. .

I usually reply that it depends on your situation and your needs. No one is in the same position, and not everyone has the necessary emergency funds in the

bank to take the plunge. But dollar for dollar, there is no greater wealth-builder than investment in the stock market.

Don't take my word for it. Dig a little into the statistics, and do the math for yourself. I'm convinced that this exercise will give you the confidence you need to begin your journey into financial freedom via the share market.

3) Lead sentence/paragraph

The lead describes the current situation, raises doubts about the future, and gets us thinking about what to do next.

4) Suggestions

"You Should"… Here the author gives us his/her opinions, provides support for their argument, and quotes the experts.

5) Conclusion

This part summarizes the advice and explains the real-life benefits.

Here is a detailed example of a financial advice column:

Section	Content	Notes
Headline	**Why The Stock Market is a Bad Long-Term Investment**	
By-line	*June 27, 2006 – Finance Daily, Bill Henrch*	
Lead	At a party recently, I was asked which stock I recommended holding until retirement. I replied that all stock investments should be sold on a regular basis. These days it is difficult for the average investor to know whether to buy or to hold is the best strategy. What should the careful investor do to ensure a wealthy retirement?	Introduces the situation (conversation at a party) Raises questions (How to invest for retirement: should I invest in stocks?)
Suggestion 1	Research Before Buying The best advice I can give is to put your money into solid companies. As Dirk Smith, president of the ABC Bank says, "If you are not comfortable with their financial situation, then you shouldn't risk your money."	"You should" (…choose companies carefully) Quotations (president of ABC Bank)
Suggestion 2	Take your profits and invest again. Too many investors hold on during bad times, hoping that the market will rebound. You only have to look at the loss of funds from 2000 onwards to see that rebounds are not guaranteed.	"You should" (…focus on short-term investments)
Conclusion	There is nothing certain in life, but a cautious attitude to stock investment will help create a solid financial base for the future.	This part is a summary of the advice (short term investment yields long term wealth).

Stock market: *Long-term investment:*

To hold stock: *To recommend:*   *Wealthy:*

Retirement: *Solid company:*   *To risk:*

Profits: *Bad times:*   *To rebound:*

Not guaranteed: *Cautious attitude:*   *Financial base:*

E) Financial Predictions

Many financial articles try to guess future interest rates and other important fiscal matters.

Future interest rates: *Fiscal matters*:

Articles like this have the following basic structure:

1) Headline ————————————→ **Will The Bulls Beat the Bears by Xmas?**

May 6 - Mohammad Chang, WebWealth, Chicago

The headline raises
the main issue
and hints at a prediction.

The recent rally in the market suggests that American stocks are nearly out of the slump that began this April. But are things really so simple?

The major indices are now trading at or above their benchmark performance at the start of the year. With superior 4th quarter earning predicted by the major players, there is room for cautious optimism.

The seasonal effect should not be discounted however. Sam Tover of Municipal Realty and Finance says that there is a natural tendency for the market to rally in the weeks just before the New Year. "We see the current

performance as a product of periodic adjustments rather than any real shift in the opinion of buyers as a whole." But Ken Edington of CityWorld disagrees. "What you are seeing in the current rally is recognition that stocks have been oversold for far too long."

Whether the current uptrend is an artifact or a phenomenon remains to be seen. As of Friday however, all three major indices were recording record highs, and posting significant volume.

2) By-line

3) Lead sentence/paragraph

The lead describes
the current situation
and the uncertain outcome.

4) Body

This section provides details,
offers opinions from experts, introduces
contrasting opinions, and provides
quotations.

5) Conclusion

The article ends with a description of the
short-term outlook.

Let's look at a financial prediction in detail:

Section	Content	Notes
Headline	**Will SOMY Dividend Increase Start a Trend?**	Introduces the issue (The large dividend increase at SOMY) Raises a question (Is this the start of a trend?)
By-line	*May 1, 2006 – Los Angeles, CN Times, Patty Karaj*	
Lead	The $20 billion increase in dividends for the quarter, announced by SOMY on Friday, has analysts wondering if this signals a change in attitude by major US corporations.	Current situation ($20 billion increase in dividends) Uncertain future (Will other companies introduce similar increases?)
Body	The announcement by SOMY followed 3 consecutive quarters of extraordinary profits by the software giant. "Other companies may need to make similar adjustments if they wish to remain competitive," said Frank Tith, president of Trans-Global Investment Trust.	Provides details (The dividend is the result of large profits.) Opinions from experts (Other companies will introduce increases.)
Body	Others however, were not convinced. The chief of the Federal Reserve Bank called the situation "an isolated incident." He believes that it is not likely to affect the market as a whole.	Contrasting opinion (No further increases) Quotation (from the Federal Reserve Bank)
Conclusion	For now, investors appear skeptical of major dividend increases. Trading volume for SOMY increased Friday following the announcement but remained average for the software industry as a whole.	Short-term outlook (No other major changes yet)

Dividend increase: *Trend*:   *Quarter*:

Analysts: *To signal*:   *Major corporations*:

Announcement: *Consecutive*:   *Extraordinary profits*:

Software giant: *Competitive*:   *Investment trust*:

Remain unconvinced: *Chief*:   *Federal Reserve*:

Isolated incident: *To affect*:   *As a whole*:

Skeptical: *Trading volume*:

139

Tips VI – Crossword

Across

3. Financial sites tell us about currency ___ rates
4. P/E is the ___ To Earnings ratio
7. EPS means ___ Per Share
9. Advice columns help us to ___
10. If a stock crashes, it goes ___
11. Financial news is about the ___ of the market

Down

1. Financial predictions guess about future ___ rates
2. ROI means Return On ___
5. A price ___ means strong upward movement
6. The ___ summarizes the article
8. The most important information is found in the ___

140

Section 3: Idiomatic Expressions (Part I)

3.1 A backlash against

Meaning: A whole group suffers (prejudice, attacks, etc.) because one of its members did something bad.

Meaning in your language:

Usage: There is a backlash against *A* (group) because of *B* (action)

1. There was <u>a backlash</u> in America <u>against</u> all Moslems after the terrorist incidents in New York.

Moslems: *Terrorist incidents (see 1.14):*

2. There was <u>a</u> strong <u>backlash against</u> the landlord after the rent hike.

Landlord: *Rent hike:*

3. There was <u>a backlash against</u> criminal investigators after the news story on kickbacks hit the airwaves.

Criminal investigators: *To hit the airwaves:*

Related expressions: To single out

A scapegoat

3.2 A bitter pill to swallow

Meaning: Something makes people sad or angry.

Meaning in your language:

Usage: *A* (something) is a bitter pill to swallow

1. The environmentalist's loss after her long, hard court battle was <u>a bitter pill to swallow</u>.

Environmentalist: *Court battle:*

2. Failing the university entrance examination was <u>a bitter pill to swallow</u>.

Entrance examination:

3. The collapse of his business was <u>a bitter pill to swallow</u>, but he still seemed optimistic.

Collapse of a business: *Optimistic:*

Related expressions: Hard to take

A bitter disappointment

3.3 A / The ... craze

Meaning: There is great excitement about something; something is very trendy.

Meaning in your language:

Usage: An **A** (topic) craze

1. Many people joined the rather expensive health club during <u>the</u> fitness <u>craze</u> last summer.

Health club: *Fitness:*

2. There is always <u>a</u> souvenir-collecting <u>craze</u> during major sporting events like the Olympics.

Souvenir-collecting: *Sporting events:*

3. <u>The</u> golfing <u>craze</u> that was everywhere in Japan during the 1980s ended with the start of the economic downturn.

Economic downturn:

Related expressions: Selling like hotcakes

Something is hot

Board shorts are the latest craze with teenagers

3.4 A flight of fancy

Meaning: Something is crazy, silly, impossible, or stupid.

Meaning in your language:

Usage: *A* (some action) is a flight of fancy

1. It was <u>a flight of fancy</u> to think that he would ever change his mind.

Change his mind:

2. The Republican called his Democratic rival's economic plan <u>a flight of fancy</u>.

Republican: *Democrat:*   *Rival:*

Economic plan:

3. Starting a small business was <u>a flight of fancy</u>. She should have kept her secure job.

Small business: *Secure job:*

Related expressions: Wishful thinking

                               Utter nonsense

3.5 A flop

Meaning: Something is a failure, or something is a disappointment.

Meaning in your language:

Usage: *A* (event, project, relationship) is a flop

1. The movie was <u>a</u> complete <u>flop</u>. Nobody went to see it.

2. The wine and cheese party was <u>a flop</u> because they ran out of wine.

Wine and cheese party: *To run out of something:*

3. The marathon was <u>a flop</u> because of the freak storm.

Marathon: *Freak storm:*

Related expressions: A dud

                              A lemon

3.6 A high-stakes...

Meaning: Something is very important, expensive, or dangerous.

Meaning in your language:

Usage: A high-stakes *A* (action)

1. Buying a new apartment before selling your previous one is <u>a high-stakes</u> gamble.

Buying an apartment: *A gamble:*

2. If you are considering running for governor, you should realized that politics is <u>a high-stakes</u> game. It is not for the timid.

Running for: *Governor:*   *Timid:*

3. <u>The stakes are high</u> at this meeting between the Israeli and the Palestinian leaders.

Israeli: *Palestinian leader:*

Related expressions: Playing for keeps

Do or die situation

3.7 A / the....hike

Meaning: The cost of something increases.

Meaning in your language:

Usage: An *A* (wage, price) hike

A hike in *A* (wage, price)

1. <u>The</u> new <u>hike</u> in the price of gasoline, scheduled from June of next year, is very bad news for car owners.

Price of gasoline: *Car owners:*

2. The world-famous race-car driver is asking for <u>a</u> wage <u>hike</u> as one of the terms in his new contract.

Race-car driver: *Term in a contract:*

3. Greengrocers always introduce <u>a</u> price <u>hike</u> for produce during the winter months.

Greengrocers: *Produce:*

Related expressions: Soaring prices

Price-gouging

3.8 A hit with

Meaning: Something is successful or entertaining.

Meaning in your language:

Usage: **A** (event, performance, person) is a hit with **B** (person, group)

1. The juggler <u>was a hit with</u> the crowd, and they kept asking for encores.

Juggler: *Encores:*

2. The new overnight train service is <u>a hit with</u> most tourists.

Overnight: *Train service:*

3. The toy <u>will</u> probably <u>be a hit with</u> younger children when it goes on sale next Friday.

To go on sale:

Related expressions: Selling like hot-cakes

A runaway success

The fondue was a hit with the guests

3.9 A / the ...-looking

Meaning: Something seems to have a certain quality or characteristic.

Meaning in your language:

Usage: An **A** (adjective)-looking **B** (person, place, thing)
1. There is <u>a</u> very hungry-<u>looking</u> dog just outside the convenience store.
Hungry: *Convenience store:*
2. <u>The</u> sad-<u>looking</u> woman told reporters that there was still no news regarding the whereabouts of her missing infant.
Whereabouts: *Missing infant:*
3. <u>A</u> very tired-<u>looking</u> mayor greeted the citizens at 2 am after the election results were known.
To greet: *Election results:*

Related expressions: A hint of

A sense of

3.10 (Only) a matter of time

Meaning: Something will probably happen (or has happened).

Meaning in your language:

Usage: It is only a matter of time before **A** (situation, result)
1. It is <u>only a matter of time</u> before those biker kids have a traffic accident.
Biker kids: *Traffic accident:*
2. It was <u>only a matter of time</u> before that new pizzeria started to attract customers.
Pizzeria: *To attract customers:*
3. Many people believe that it's <u>only a matter of time</u> before a solution is found to the energy crisis.
To find a solution: *Energy crisis:*

Related expressions: In due course

To end up in

3.11 A / the ... measure

Meaning: A plan, policy, or action

Meaning in your language:

Usage: An **A** (policy, goal) measure

1. The latest cost-cutting measure from the auditor is to reduce salaries for employees by 2%.

Auditor: *Cost-cutting:*

Salary reduction:

2. The foreign workers complained that the company's anti-discrimination measures are ineffective.

Foreign workers: *Anti-discrimination:*

Ineffective:

3. Water restrictions were introduced as a water conservation measure in this municipality last year.

Water restrictions: *Municipality:*

Related expressions: To come to grips with

Come to terms with

3.12 A meeting of the minds

Meaning: Two people reach an agreement, or really understand each other.

Meaning in your language:

Usage: There is a meeting of the minds between **A** (person, group) and **B** (person, group)

1. The ambassador is hoping for a meeting of the minds with his counterpart at the next summit.

Ambassador: *Counterpart:*   *Summit:*

2. If there is no meeting of the minds regarding trade sanctions, it may sour the relationship between the countries.

Trade sanctions: *To sour a relationship:*

3. A meeting of the minds may be impossible with her because she is a mean-spirited person.

Mean-spirited person:

Related expressions: To make headway

To see eye to eye

148

3.13 An eyesore

Meaning: Something is ugly or hard to look at.

Meaning in your language:

Usage: *A* (some object) is an eyesore

1. That purple tie is really <u>an eyesore</u>. You should change it before you go to your interview with the comptroller.

Purple tie: *Comptroller:*

2. That building is <u>an eyesore</u>. I wish some developer would tear it down.

Developer: *To tear down a building:*

3. The harbor was <u>an eyesore</u> before the redevelopment project started.

Harbor: *Redevelopment project:*

Related expressions: To clash (2 colors)

A white elephant

That apartment is an eyesore

3.14 (An) up and comer

Meaning: Someone is becoming well-known very quickly.

Meaning in your language:

Usage: *A* (person) is an up and comer

1. ABC company is <u>an up and comer</u> in the pharmaceutical business. Its new cold medicine is selling very quickly.

Pharmaceutical business: *Cold medicine:*

2. This <u>up and comer</u> in the boxing world could be a real threat at the championships next year.

Boxing world: *A real threat:*

Championships:

3. The success of his new exhibition makes him <u>an up and comer</u> on the art scene.

Exhibition: *Art scene:*

Related expressions: A rising star

Talk of the town

3.15 Anyone's guess

Meaning: The future is uncertain; nobody knows how something will end

Meaning in your language:

Usage: *A* (fact) is anyone's guess

1. The baseball game is very close and it's <u>anyone's guess</u> who will win.

A close game:

2. It's <u>anyone's guess</u> whether the food supplies will arrive from overseas in time to save the children.

Food supplies: *From overseas:*

In time:

3. Whether the new company will succeed or not in this competitive marketplace is <u>anyone's guess</u>.

Competitive marketplace:

Related expressions: A cliffhanger

Could go either way

3.16 A setback in / to

Meaning: Life has become difficult because of something.

Meaning in your language:

Usage: *A* (event) is a setback to *B* (person, group, plan)

1. The pianist's terrible performance yesterday is <u>a setback in</u> his plans to win the piano competition.

Pianist: *Performance:*

2. The plane crash was <u>a</u> major <u>setback to</u> the new freight company.

Plane crash: *Freight company:*

3. Although the volunteer organization will continue with the fund-raising campaign, the scandal is certainly <u>a</u> major <u>setback</u>.

Volunteer organization: *Fund-raising campaign:*

Related expressions: A fly in the ointment

A blow to

3.17 (Off to) a shaky / bad start

Meaning: Something begins badly.

Meaning in your language:

Usage: *A* (person, group) is off to a shaky start

1. The tennis tournament is <u>off to a bad start</u> because the best player practiced too much and got tennis elbow.

Tournament: *Tennis elbow:*

2. His election campaign is <u>off to a shaky start</u> because of a lack of funds.

Election campaign: *Lack of funds:*

3. Sales of his new CD were <u>off to a shaky start</u>, but have recently improved.

CD Sales:

Related expressions: Off on the wrong foot

An ill omen

151

3.18 A slim chance (of)

Meaning: Something is probably not going to happen; something is not likely

Meaning in your language:

Usage: There is a slim chance of **A** (event)

1. There is <u>a slim chance of</u> rain between now and the weekend.

2. There is only <u>a slim chance</u> that he will recover from his serious accident.

To recover: *Serious accident:*

3. If there is even <u>a slim chance of</u> success, then the negotiations between the countries should continue.

Success: *Negotiations:*

Related expressions: A snowball's chance in hell

A fat chance

3.19 A ....streak

Meaning #1: Someone has a special emotional style or character trait.

Meaning in your language:

Usage: **A** (person, animal) has a **B** (character trait) streak in him/her.

1. He has <u>a</u> stubborn <u>streak</u> that sometimes gets him into trouble with his coworkers.

Stubborn: *To get into trouble:*

2. His teachers say he has <u>a</u> rebellious <u>streak</u> in him.

Rebellious:

Meaning #2: <to streak>: Someone runs naked through a public place

Meaning in your language:

1. The teenagers shocked the elderly people <u>by streaking</u> down the aisle.

Elderly people: *To shock:*   *The aisle:*

2. The man was arrested <u>for streaking</u> during the rock concert.

To be arrested: *Rock concert:*

Related expressions: A touch of something (Meaning #1)

Buck-naked (Meaning #2)

3.20 A war of words

Meaning: A public argument between two groups or people

Meaning in your language:

Usage: There is a war of words between **A** (person, group) and **B** (person, group)

1. The <u>war of words</u> between the two famous conductors is really embarrassing for the opera house management.

Conductor: *Opera house:*

2. If this <u>war of words</u> between the tiny African nations continues, it may lead to armed conflict.

Tiny nations: *Armed conflict:*

3. The <u>war of words</u> between the married couple started long before their divorce.

Married couple: *Divorce:*

Related expressions: Trading barbs

                                Back-biting

3.21 A / The…wave (of)

Meaning: A sudden/strong increase in the amount of something

Meaning in your language:

Usage: The wave of **A** (objects, people, actions) is **B** (result, opinion)

1. <u>The</u> recent crime <u>wave</u> has led the mayor to recruit more police officers.

To recruit:

2. The bank president said that <u>the</u> recent <u>wave of</u> applications for house loans was a sign of new economic growth.

Bank president: *House loans:*

Economic growth:

3. I was overcome by <u>a wave of</u> emotion when I saw my newborn baby.

Overcome by: *Newborn baby:*

Related expressions: A string of

                                A series of

3.22 A whole different ballgame

Meaning: The situation has completely changed.

Meaning in your language:

Usage: It would be a whole different ballgame if/when **A** (event, situation)

1. I can't afford that car, but it would be <u>a whole different ballgame</u> if I were rich.

Can't afford: *To be rich:*

2. It will be <u>a whole different ballgame</u> for the elderly if doctors discover a wonder drug for arthritis.

The elderly: *Wonder drug:*   *Arthritis:*

3. If you had studied harder for the bar exam, it would have been <u>a whole different ballgame</u>.

Bar exam:

Related expressions: A different kettle of fish

Another story

3.23 A win-win situation

Meaning: Everybody is happy with some result.

Meaning in your language:

Usage: **A** (fact, circumstances) is a win-win situation

1. The end of the negotiations is <u>a win-win situation</u> for both employees and management.

Negotiations: *Employees:*   *Management:*

2. If the war ends, it will be <u>a win-win situation</u> for both nations.

Both nations:

3. New urban development would be <u>a win-win situation</u> for both the business community and for the residents of the town.

Urban development: *Business community:*

Residents of the town:

Related expressions: An equitable agreement

A done-deal

3.24 Believed to be / that

Meaning: Someone is making a guess about something.

Meaning in your language:

Usage: *A* (person, group, object, event) is believed to be *B* (description)

1. This month's jackpot is <u>believed to be</u> the largest amount in the history of the national lottery.

Jackpot: *National lottery:*

Largest in history:

2. He is <u>believed to be</u> the man responsible for the terrible murder.

Responsible for: *Terrible murder:*

3. It is <u>believed that</u> the necklace is made from pure gold.

Necklace: *Pure gold:*

Related expression: Common knowledge

                                 Thought to be

3.25 Beyond (me)

Meaning: Something is confusing, hard to believe, or hard to understand.

Meaning in your language:

Usage: It is beyond me why *A* (fact, situation, decision)

1. It's <u>beyond me</u> why he chose to get married to such a difficult woman.

To get married to: *Difficult woman:*

2. Why the bank hired him is <u>beyond me</u>! He's a very lazy man.

To be hired: *Lazy man:*

3. The police chief said it was <u>beyond him</u> why the suspect was released after questioning by the officer.

Police chief: *The suspect:*

Released after questioning:

Related expressions: It's all Greek to me

                                 Escapes me

3.26 Booked / booked up / booked solid

Meaning: A service is so popular that it is now unavailable.

Meaning in your language:

Usage: The (place, service) is booked up

1. All of the cheap flights to Hawaii are already totally <u>booked</u> because this is the busy season.

Cheap flights:

2. I wanted to eat at that new vegetarian restaurant, but they're <u>booked solid</u> for today.

Vegetarian restaurant: *Booked solid:*

3. Airline passengers stranded by the typhoon found that all the hotels were <u>booked up</u>.

Stranded passengers: *Typhoon:*

Related expressions: Sold out

  Jam packed

3.27 Bound to (be)

Meaning: Something is almost certain to happen.

Meaning in your language:

Usage: *A* (person, group, situation) is bound to *B* (action) because *C* (reason)

1. That bus line is <u>bound to</u> do well. They provide passengers with good service at reasonable prices.

Bus line: *Good service:*

Reasonable prices:

2. He's such a big star that his latest movie is <u>bound to</u> make millions.

Big star:

3. The pileup this morning is no surprise to me. There was <u>bound to be</u> an accident at that dangerous intersection someday.

Pileup: *Dangerous intersection:*

Related expressions: Odds are....

  Dollars to donuts

156

3.28 Calls for

Meaning: People are demanding something.
Meaning in your language:

Usage: There are calls for *A* (action)

A (person, group) is calling for *B* (action)

1. There were <u>calls for</u> the teacher's resignation by angry parents after his gambling addiction became public.

Resignation: *Gambling addiction:*

Became public:

2. The under secretary is expected to <u>call for</u> a free trade agreement at the next trade summit.

Under secretary: *Free trade agreement:*

Trade summit:

3. There were <u>calls for</u> a recount because it was such a close election.

A recount: *Close election:*

Related expressions: To lobby

The voice of the people

3.29 Cause for alarm

Meaning: Some news is shocking or frightening.
Meaning in your language:

Usage: *A* (news, fact) is cause for alarm.

1. The increase in small earthquakes in the surrounding area is really a <u>cause for alarm</u>.

Small earthquakes: *Surrounding area:*

2. The meteorologists say that ozone layer depletion is <u>cause for alarm</u>.

Meteorologists: *Ozone layer:*   *Depletion:*

3. The shortage of basic medical supplies in that part of Asia is <u>cause for alarm</u>.

Shortage: *Medical supplies:*

Related expressions: A wake-up call

To give pause for thought

3.30 Considered

Meaning: Someone has a viewpoint/opinion about something.

Meaning in your language:

Usage: **A** (topic) is considered **B** (opinion, viewpoint)

1. According to the news bulletin, the escaped criminal is armed, and is <u>considered</u> extremely dangerous.

News bulletin: *Escaped criminal:*

To be armed:

2. It is <u>considered</u> likely that Canada will win the Gold in ice skating at the Olympics this year.

Likely: *Win the Gold:*   *Ice skating:*

3. The specialist said that this medicine is <u>considered</u> the best choice for treatment of the infection.

Specialist: *Treatment of the infection:*

Related expressions: As far as ... is concerned

Thought to be

3.31 Cream of the crop

Meaning: Something is the best; of very high quality.

Meaning in your language:

Usage: **A** (person, group, object) is the cream of the crop

1. It is common knowledge that students in that graduate program are <u>the cream of the crop</u>.

Common knowledge: *Graduate program:*

2. <u>The cream of the crop</u> competes fiercely every four years in the Olympics.

To compete fiercely:

3. All of the general practitioners at the health center are good, but he is <u>the cream of the crop</u>.

General practitioners: *Health center:*

Related expressions: As good as it gets

Crème de la crème

3.32 Duped (into)

Meaning: Someone fools or cheats someone else.

Meaning in your language:

Usage: *A* (person) is duped into *B* (action) by *C* (person, group)

1. He <u>was duped into</u> buying the useless product by the door-to-door salesman.

Useless product: *Door-to-door salesman:*

2. The used car salesman tried <u>to dupe</u> the young couple <u>into</u> buying a broken-down automobile.

Used car salesman: *Young couple:*

Broken-down automobile:

3. The plastics factory <u>duped</u> the ecologists by promising them environmental reforms at a later date.

Plastics factory: *Ecologists:*

Environmental reforms:

Related expressions: Lead one down the garden path

Pull of wool over one's eyes

3.33 Fast approaching

Meaning: Something is coming soon.

Meaning in your language:

Usage: *A* (event, situation) is fast approaching

1. Even though the average temperature is still low, it's already March and spring is <u>fast approaching</u>.

Average temperature:

2. The deadline for university applications is <u>fast approaching</u>. You'd better hurry!

Deadline: *University application:*

3. The general told his press entourage that time for action is <u>fast approaching</u>.

General: *Press entourage:*

Time for action:

Related expressions: Before you know it

Any day now

3.34 Left and right

Meaning: At many places; by many people; in many directions

Meaning in your language:

> **Usage**: **A** (person, group, organization) is **B** (action) from left and right
>
> 1. The swim team coach was criticized from left and right for letting his swimmers take drugs.
>
> *Swim team coach:*   *To take drugs:*
>
> 2. Missiles bombarded the town from left and right, in what was the heaviest attack since the beginning of the war.
>
> *Missiles:*   *To bombard:*   *Heavy attack:*
>
> 3. The taxi driver swerved left and right, trying to get the minister to the wedding on time.
>
> *To swerve:*   *Minister:*

Related expressions: From all sides

On all fronts

3.35 Grassroots

Meaning: Something is created by ordinary people, rather than by government or big business.

Meaning in your language:

> **Usage**: A grassroots **A** (organization, activity)
>
> 1. The relief efforts in Africa started with grassroots activities by a few volunteers.
>
> *Relief efforts:*   *Volunteers:*
>
> 2. The profits from the classical music concert are being donated to a few grassroots organizations.
>
> *Classical music concert:*   *To donate:*
>
> 3. Grassroots movements are growing through the use of the internet.

Related expressions: A groundswell

Pulling together

3.36 If you ask me

Meaning: My opinion is... / from my perspective…

Meaning in your language:

Usage: If you ask me, **A** (opinion)

1. <u>If you ask me</u>, the government's new economic policy is just not good enough.

Economic policy: *Not good enough:*

2. I'm glad you like the shirt, but <u>if you ask me</u>, the color's a little bold...

A little bold:

3. <u>If you ask me</u>, I think that the surgeon should resign to take responsibility for his actions.

Surgeon: *To resign:*

To take responsibility for something:

Related expressions: If it were up to me

My slant on the matter

That's a great hotel, if you ask me

3.37 In (full) swing

Meaning: Some event is very busy; something is doing well

Meaning in your language:

Usage: *A* (product) is in full swing

1. The Flower Festival is <u>in full swing</u> and the visitors are really enjoying themselves.

Flower Festival: *To enjoy oneself:*

2. Once you get <u>into the swing</u> of your new job, I think you will really do well.

3. The blood drive is <u>in full swing</u>, and there are many nurses in the square looking for volunteers.

Blood drive: *Nurses:*

Related expressions: Selling like hot cakes

A roaring success

3.38 In the cards

Meaning: Something will probably happen.

Meaning in your language:

Usage: *A* (plan) is in the cards

1. The supervisor told the employee that a company car was <u>in the cards</u> if he continued to work diligently.

Supervisor: *Diligently:*

2. Many people believe that an international agreement on greenhouse gas emission targets is <u>in the cards</u>.

International agreement: *Greenhouse gas:*

Emission targets:

3. NASA says that a trip to Mars in the near future is <u>in the cards</u>.

Trip to Mars:

Related expressions: In the bag

In the works

162

3.39 In the crosshairs

Meaning: Something is the focus of attention.

Meaning in your language:

Usage: *A* (topic, person, organization, plan) is in the crosshairs

1. The controversial antismoking bill will be <u>in the crosshairs</u> at the next town meeting.

Controversial: *Antismoking:*

Bill:

2. The congress member's strange behavior before her election is now <u>in the crosshairs</u>.

Congress member: *Strange behavior:*

3. <u>In the crosshairs</u> at the press conference was the baseball manager's plan to hire a foreign coach.

Press conference: *Baseball manager:*

Foreign coach:

Related expressions: Under the microscope

                                     Under scrutiny

Mini-Quiz: Expressions Part I

Part A

1. That talented young player is considered … in the baseball world.
a) a whole different ballgame **b)** an up and comer **c)** from left and right **d)** in the cards

2. Many people are …. buying worthless jewelry by the man on the mall.
a) believed to be   **b)** considered   **c)** calls for   **d)** duped into

3. The volunteer network started from just a few …. organizations.
a) flight of fancy   **b)** crosshairs   **c)** in full swing   **d)** grassroots

4. The school is introducing the recycling of textbooks as a cost-cutting ....
a) measure   **b)** flop   **c)** meeting of the minds   **d)** up and comer

5. Signing that deal puts both companies in…
a) a high-stakes   **b)** a good-looking   **c)** a slim chance   **d)** a win-win situation

6. Many people started exercising every day during last year's .....
a) in the crosshairs   **b)** fitness craze   **c)** anyone's guess   **d)** fast approaching

7...... immigrants is expected because of the outbreak of war.
a) A wave of   **b)** If you ask me   **c)** A tennis craze   **d)** A hit with

8.He is very talented and it is only …before he becomes famous.
a) anyone's guess   **b)** considered   **c)** a matter of time   **d)** bound to

9.Hurry to the branch nearest you. Remember, the end of the sale is …
a) in the cards   **b)** considered   **c)** a winning streak   **d)** fast approaching

10. That new videogame is … kids under 12.
a) a hit with   **b)** in full swing   **c)** cause for alarm   **d)** beyond me

11. The … will be appearing in the all-star basketball game this Saturday.
a) war of words   **b)** cream of the crop   **c)** backlash against   **d)** meeting of the minds

12. She really likes him. I think that a new romance is …
a) in the cards   **b)** an eyesore   **c)** beyond me   **d)** a flight of fancy

13. There is only a … of rain tomorrow.
a) matter of time   **b)** backlash against   **c)** slim chance   **d)** win-win situation

14. Why our teacher is acting so emotional these days is…
a) in the cards   **b)** totally booked   **c)** a war of words   **d)** anyone's guess

15. The blood donation campaign is now …
a) believed to be   **b)** in full swing   **c)** a bitter pill to swallow   **d)** cream of the crop

Part B

1. An up	a. crosshairs
2. From left	b. ask me
3. A backlash	c. different ballgame
4. In the	d. to swallow
5. A whole	e. of fancy
6. A flight	f. and comer
7. If you	g. of words
8. A win	h. chance of
9. Cream of	i. against
10. A meeting	j. of the minds
11. In full	k. the crop
12. Cause for	l. win situation
13. A war	m. and right
14. A slim	n. swing
15. A bitter pill	o. alarm

Part C

E.g. may / that / as / be / it : <u>Be that as it may</u>

1. pill / bitter / a / to / swallow : _____
2. fancy / flight / of / a : _____
3. a / the / of / minds / meeting : _____
4. up / an / and / comer : _____
5. chance / a / slim / of : _____
6. a / of / words / war : _____
7. a / different / whole / ballgame : _____
8. cream / crop / the / of : _____
9. if / me / you / ask : _____
10. cards / in / the : _____

TIPS VII: Sporting News Websites

Here are some of the best places online to read about sports:

Company	Website	Notes
CBS	www.sportsline.com	Run by CBS, an American media giant. the same company provides the websites for NCAA sports and the NFL
ESPN	espn.go.com	Entertainment and Sports Programming Network, also on American cable television
Fox Sports	msn.foxsports.com	Part of the Fox Broadcasting Company, an American media giant.
Sports Illustrated	sportsillustrated.cnn.com	Famous sports magazine (combined with CNN) owned by Time Warner
Sports Network, The	www.sportsnetwork.com	Part of TSN, a major Canadian media giant, and similar to ESPN
Sporting News	www.sportingnews.com	Major sports website, run by American City Business Journals, Inc.
Topix	www.topix.net/sports	International sporting news site
Yahoo Sports	sports.yahoo.com	Owned by Yahoo! Inc., a major internet service provider

Media giant:

NCAA=National Collegiate Athletic Association; *NFL*=National Football League

And here are some websites dealing with particular sports.

Company	Website	Notes
ARU	www.rugby.com.au	For Australian rugby fans
FIFA	www.fifa.com	All the news on football*, including the World Cup
MLB	www.mlb.com	Major League Baseball (USA)
Nascar	www.nascar.com	Stock Car Auto Racing (USA)
NBA	www.nba.com	This is the official website for the National Basketball Association (USA)
NFL	www.nfl.com	This is the official website for the National Football League (USA)
NHL	www.nlh.com	The official site for the National Hockey League (North America)
USGA	www.usga.org	United States Golf Association

*Note: European "football" is called "soccer" in many countries

TIPS VIII: Understanding Online Sporting News

A) <u>Basic Structure of a Sporting News Website</u>

Most sporting news websites have the following primary elements:

1) General sports news

2) Features
(Game-deciding moves,
key-player interviews,
score tables)

3) Links to related pages

4) Upcoming events

Ireland Topples Australia 3−Nil

Up Close and Personal With Rodriguez

Click here for an NBA recap

Click here for NHL schedules

QB Out with Hamstring Injury

5) Lists of injuries

6) Photos

B) Key Vocabulary

1) Sports Organizations Continued (See TIPS VII)

Here are some common acronyms for sports organizations:

Acronym	Sports Organization	Your Language
FIFA	Federation Internationale de Football Association	
Formula One	Formula One	
IBF	International Boxing Federation	
IOC	International Olympic Committee	
MLB	Major League Baseball	
NASCAR	National Association for Stock Car Auto Racing	
NBA	National Basketball Association	
NFL	National Football League	
NHL	National Hockey League	
PGA	Professional Golfer's Association	
Tour de France	Tour de France	
WTA	Women's Tennis Association	
WTF	World Taekwondo Federation	
WWE	World Wrestling Entertainment	

2) Sports Vocabulary

Many sports have their own special vocabulary. Here is a list of some words used in the game of baseball.

Common baseball terminology:

English Nouns	Your Language
Ball	
Batter	
Bleachers	
Catcher	
Dugout	
First base	
Home plate	
Home run	
Out	
Pitcher	
Strike	
The Majors	

English Verbs	Your Language
To bunt	
To catch	
To fumble (a ball)	
To pitch	
To slide	
To steal (a base)	
To strike out	
To walk	

3) Emotive Vocabulary (a feature of sports news articles)

Here is a list of some colorful, emotive sports vocabulary:

English Term	Your Language	Sample Sentence
Break free		The QB broke free to score a touchdown. *QB*: *Touchdown*:
Counterattack		The counterattack was highly impressive. *Impressive*:
Flailing		The goalie's flailing came to naught. *To come to naught*:
Penetrating		The penetrating attack won the game.
Primo		Johnson is the primo starter this season. *Starter*:
Rain down		Balls rained down on the goalie in the latter half of the game. *Goalie*: *Latter half*:
Savior		Martins is truly the team's savior.
Stung		The French team was stung by the defeat. *Defeat*:

C) <u>Sports Articles</u>

1) General Sports News

General sports news has a similar structure to general news articles.

Primary Elements:

1. Headline

2. By-line

3. Lead

(1st sentence/sometimes
1st paragraph)

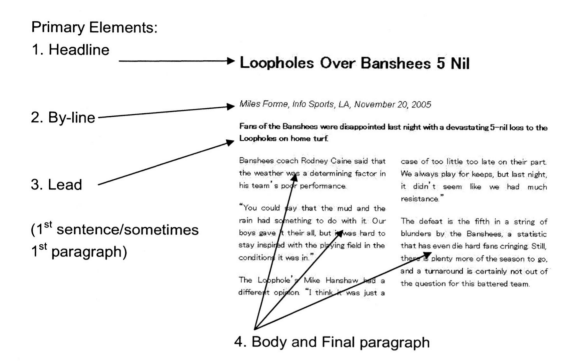

Loopholes Over Banshees 5 Nil

Miles Forme, Info Sports, LA, November 20, 2005

Fans of the Banshees were disappointed last night with a devastating 5-nil loss to the Loopholes on home turf.

Banshees coach Rodney Caine said that the weather was a determining factor in his team's poor performance.

"You could say that the mud and the rain had something to do with it. Our boys gave it their all, but it was hard to stay inspired with the playing field in the conditions it was in."

The Loophole's Mike Hanshaw had a different opinion. "I think it was just a case of too little too late on their part. We always play for keeps, but last night, it didn't seem like we had much resistance."

The defeat is the fifth in a string of blunders by the Banshees, a statistic that has even die hard fans cringing. Still, there is plenty more of the season to go, and a turnaround is certainly not out of the question for this battered team.

4. Body and Final paragraph

D) <u>Sports Features</u>

Primary Elements:

1.) Headline

Short, colorful words

2.) By-line

3.) Lead

Grabs attention,
often describes a key
moment in a game

4.) Core

The core provides
the point of the article

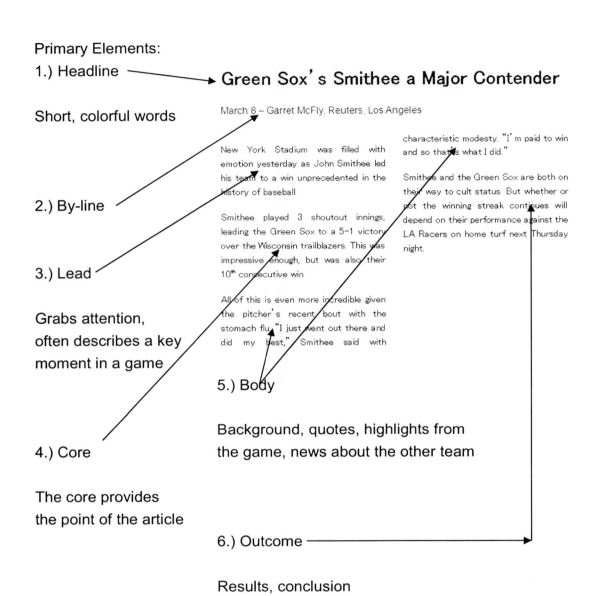

Green Sox's Smithee a Major Contender

March 8 – Garret McFly, Reuters, Los Angeles

New York Stadium was filled with emotion yesterday as John Smithee led his team to a win unprecedented in the history of baseball.

Smithee played 3 shoutout innings, leading the Green Sox to a 5-1 victory over the Wisconsin trailblazers. This was impressive enough, but was also their 10th consecutive win.

All of this is even more incredible given the pitcher's recent bout with the stomach flu. "I just went out there and did my best," Smithee said with characteristic modesty. "I'm paid to win and so that's what I did."

Smithee and the Green Sox are both on their way to cult status. But whether or not the winning streak continues will depend on their performance against the LA Racers on home turf next Thursday night.

5.) Body

Background, quotes, highlights from
the game, news about the other team

6.) Outcome

Results, conclusion

174

Here is a sample of a sports feature:

Section	Content	Notes
Headline	**Hawk's Fernandez a Force of Nature**	Fernandez = player Hawk = team Force of Nature = impressive
By-line	*February 3, 2006 – Reuters, Boston, Guy Peterson*	
Lead	From the mood of the crowd at Boston Stadium last night, it seems like the Hawks and their star player can do no wrong this season.	This puts us into the game.
Core	Star pitcher Fernandez had five shutout innings, leading his team to a 6-2 victory over the Canaries.	Canaries = other team
Body	The pitcher's numbers are all the more impressive given his recent knee injury. "I wasn't sure I could play, but if I did, I knew I would give it 100%," Fernandez said.	Background on the player
Outcome	This was the 4th win for the Hawks in inter-league games this season, placing them in fine shape ahead of their next game in Kansas on Friday night.	Results of the game, and the team's future

Mood: *Shutout*:   *Inning*:

Victory: *Numbers*:   *Impressive*:

Injury: *Inter-league*:

In fine shape: *Ahead of something*:

Tips VIII – Crossword

Across

3. Baseball term: home ___
6. NFL: ___ Football League
7. Provides the point of the article
9. NHL: National ___ League
10. MLB: Major League ___

Down

1. IOC: International ___ Committee
2. Baseball term: to ___ a base
3. PGA: ___ Golfer's Association
4. ___ sometimes give score tables
5. IBF: International ___ Federation
8. This part of an article gives highlights of the game

Section 3: Idiomatic Expressions (Part II)

3.40 Just around the corner

Meaning: Something (usually good) will probably happen soon.

Meaning in your language:

Usage: *A* (situation) is just around the corner

1. The economist told the interviewer that a fiscal recovery is <u>just around the corner</u>.

Economist: *Fiscal recovery:*

2. It's become so warm lately. Summer must be <u>just around the corner</u>.

3. That young man is such a hard-worker that I'm sure fame and fortune are <u>just around the corner</u> for him.

Hard-worker: *Fame:*

Related expressions: To be in the air

Before one knows it

New Year's Eve is just around the corner

3.41 Mud-slinging

Meaning: Someone insults or criticizes someone else unfairly.

Meaning in your language:

Usage: There is mud slinging between **A** (person, group) and **B** (person, group)

1. There has been a lot of <u>mud-slinging</u> between the campaigners during this primary.

Campaigners: *Primary (election):*

2. I think that the <u>mud-slinging</u> between the rival companies is really unprofessional.

Rival companies: *Unprofessional:*

3. In this year's cabinet sessions there has been too much <u>mud-slinging</u> and not enough intelligent debate of the issues.

Cabinet sessions: *Intelligent debate:*

Related expressions: Name-calling

                              Back-biting

3.42 No comment

Meaning: Someone doesn't want to tell a reporter something.

Meaning in your language:

Usage: **A** (person, group) has no comment regarding **B** (topic)

1. In the interview, the studio mogul had <u>no comment</u> regarding his decision to fire the director from his new movie.

Studio mogul: *Director:*

2. NASA had <u>no comment</u> regarding whether the shuttle launch would be delayed by the bad weather.

Shuttle launch: *To be delayed:*

3. Although the reporters asked the tennis ace repeatedly about her drug use, all she would say was "<u>no comment</u>."

Tennis ace: *Ask repeatedly:*

Related expressions: To keep one's mouth shut

                              To keep a lid on it

3.43 No stranger to

Meaning: Someone is very familiar with something.

Meaning in your language:

Usage: **A** (person, group) is no stranger to **B** (experience)

1. The rap star is <u>no stranger to</u> controversy. Last year's album was also strongly criticized by parents.

Rap star: *Controversy:*   *Criticized:*

2. She is <u>no stranger to</u> tragedy. Both of her parents were killed when she was still a child.

Tragedy:

3. That artist is <u>no stranger to</u> adversity. He has yet to sell a painting.

Artist: *Adversity:*

Related expressions: To be second nature
                                        Like the back of one' hand

That soldier is no stranger to conflict

180

3.44 Not worth...

Meaning: Something is of low quality or unimportant; some action is not recommended

Meaning in your language:

Usage: It is not worth **A** (action)

1. That exhibit by amateur photographers is really <u>not worth</u> seeing, in my opinion.

Exhibit: *Amateur:*   *Photographers:*

2. It is <u>not worth</u> fighting with someone if you can just give them what they want.

3. She said she wished to resign because it was <u>not worth</u> working in a high-stress office, even if the salary was high.

To resign: *High stress:*

Related expressions: Ill-advised

Beneath one

3.45 No wonder that

Meaning: The result is natural, or the result is expected.

Meaning in your language:

Usage: It is no wonder that **A** (result)

With **A** (situation), it is no wonder that **B** (result)

1. It is <u>no wonder that</u> her book is selling well. The publishing company has been really promoting it for the past few months.

Selling well: *Publishing company:*

To promote something:

2. It is <u>no wonder that</u> the athletics coach was fired. His team hadn't won for more than a year.

Athletics coach:

3. With the lack of safety at that factory, it's <u>no wonder that</u> the accident happened.

Lack of safety:

Related expressions: To serve someone right

Par for the course

3.46 Off base

Meaning: Some information is completely wrong.

Meaning in your language:

Usage: *A* (person, comments) is off base

1. His remarks were both unkind and completely <u>off base</u>.

Remarks: *Unkind:*

2. The judge dismissed the case because the prosecution's argument was completely <u>off base</u>.

Judge: *To dismiss a case:*

The prosecution:

3. The celebrity fired her publicity manager because the information he gave to the press was <u>off base</u>.

Celebrity: *Publicity manager:*

Related expressions: Not even close

                              Off the mark

3.47 Off the cuff

Meaning: Someone talks without thinking or preparation.

Meaning in your language:

Usage: ...off the cuff *A* (comments, opinions)

1. The deputy prime minister is much better than the leader of the opposition at giving <u>off the cuff</u> speeches.

Deputy prime minister:

2. Her <u>off the cuff</u> comments at the office meeting offended her boss and alienated her from her peers.

To offend: *To alienate:*   *Peers:*

3. The defense attorney gave the reporters a very moving <u>off the cuff</u> speech outside of the courthouse.

Defense attorney: *Moving:*   *Courthouse:*

Related expressions: Impromptu speech

                              To wing it

182

3.48 On a limited basis

Meaning: To test-market something, or to try something for a short time
Meaning in your language:

> **Usage:**   **A** (goods, service) are **B** (action) on a limited basis
>
> 1. The souvenirs are on sale <u>on a limited basis</u> at some stores until the day of the match.
>
> *Day of the match:*
>
> 2. He agreed to teach the class <u>on a limited basis</u> until they could find a full-time replacement.
>
> *Full-time replacement:*
>
> 3. The movie theater is offering free parking <u>on a limited basis</u> but only for the physically challenged.
>
> *Movie theater:*   *Free parking:*
>
> *The physically challenged:*

Related expressions: To give something a whirl
                                    Stick a toe in the water

3.49 On cloud nine

Meaning: Someone is very excited or happy.
Meaning in your language:

> **Usage:**   **A** (person) is on cloud nine because/since **B** (event, reason)
>
> 1. The mayor has been <u>on cloud nine</u> since his budget proposal was accepted.
>
> *Budget proposal:*
>
> 2. The general manager of the software corporation is <u>on cloud nine</u> because of the merger with Somy.
>
> *General manager:*   *Software corporation:*
>
> *Merger:*
>
> 3. The restaurant owner was <u>on cloud nine</u> until his talented chef quit.
>
> *Restaurant owner:*   *Talented chef:*

Related expressions: Happy as a clam
                                    The cat's meow

3.50 Only a / in...

Meaning: Something or someone has a special skill or quality.

Meaning in your language:

Usage: Only in *A* (place) could *B* (skill, quality)

Only an *A* (member of a group) could *B* (special quality)

1. <u>Only in</u> America would you receive such large servings of food in a restaurant.

A serving:

2. <u>Only a</u> tax accountant could solve your financial problems.

Tax accountant: *Financial problems:*

3. I think <u>only a</u> rocket scientist would be able to operate this DVD player!

Rocket scientist: *DVD player:*

Related expressions: The one and only

One of a kind

3.51 On / in the hot seat

Meaning: Someone is in a difficult situation, or has to answer criticism.

Meaning in your language:

Usage: *A* (person, organization) is in the hot seat for/over *B* (reason)

1. The company was <u>in the hot seat</u> over its plans to build a chemical plant near the mall.

Plans: *Chemical plant:*   *Mall:*

2. The actor was <u>on the hot seat</u> after criticizing the director at the Oscars.

To criticize: *Director:*   *The Oscars:*

3. The activist is <u>in the hot seat</u> for opposing the death penalty.

Activist: *To oppose something:*

Death penalty:

Related expressions: In hot water over

Feeling the heat over

3.52 On the loose

Meaning: A person (or animal) is free now, but should be arrested (or stopped).
Meaning in your language:

Usage: *A* (bad person, thing) is on the loose

1. The pedophile is still <u>on the loose</u>, and parents are advised to keep their young children safely indoors.

Pedophile: *Are advised to:*   *Indoors:*

2. The leopard that escaped from the zoo is no longer <u>on the loose</u>. It was captured this morning.

Leopard: *Captured:*

3. I don't feel safe knowing that the robber is still <u>on the loose</u>.

Robber:

Related expressions: On the run

On a rampage

3.53 On the rise

Meaning: Something is increasing.
Meaning in your language:

Usage: *A* (activity) is on the rise

1. Crime is <u>on the rise</u> in almost every urban center.

Crime: *Urban center:*

2. The tourism industry is doing well because the number of international travelers is <u>on the rise</u>.

Tourism industry: *International travelers:*

3. The number of high-end coffee shops is <u>on the rise</u>.

High end:

Related expressions: An upswing

A dime a dozen

3.54 Open to

Meaning #1: Describing the target audience for a contest, competition or club

Meaning in your language:

Usage: *A* (contest, competition, club) is open to *B* (race, group)

1. The photo contest is <u>open to</u> professional photographers between the ages of 18 and 34.

Contest: *Professional:*

2. The sorority is only <u>open to</u> female college students.

Sorority: *College students:*

Meaning #2: Someone is flexible and willing to listen.

Meaning in your language:

1. The dean said he is <u>open to</u> the possibility of changing to a co-educational system.

Dean: *Co-educational system:*

2. The investors are <u>open to</u> suggestions regarding the best site for the new dockyards.

Investors: *Dockyards:*

Related expressions: Now accepting (Meaning #1)

                                     Open-minded (Meaning #2)

"I'm open to going for a coffee with you after work"

3.55 Out of the question

Meaning: Something is impossible or shouldn't happen.
Meaning in your language:

> **Usage:** *A* (action) is out of the question
>
> 1. Asking for time off from work during the busy Xmas and New Year's season is totally <u>out of the question</u>.
>
> *Asking for time off:*   *Busy season:*
>
> 2. Even if you have plans, going out in this typhoon is <u>out of the question</u>. Just stay indoors and keep safe.
>
> *Typhoon:*   *Stay indoors:*   *Keep safe:*
>
> 3. The teacher told me that taking the test again is <u>out of the question</u> unless I have a doctor's note.
>
> *Taking the test again:*   *Doctor's note:*

Related expressions: Over my dead body

Don't even think of ....

3.56 Over time

Meaning: Something is slowly changing.
Meaning in your language:

> **Usage:** Over time, *A* (changing situation)
>
> Note: "over time" does not equal overtime (working late at the office).
>
> 1. I was worried, but <u>over time</u>, my daughter has changed from a bashful child into an outgoing young woman.
>
> *Bashful child:*   *Outgoing:*
>
> 2. When I first came to Japan, I hated sushi and many other uncooked delicacies, but <u>over time</u>, I have learned to like them.
>
> *Delicacy:*   *To learn to like something:*
>
> 3. Those schoolboys are not friends now, but might become friends <u>over time</u>.
>
> *Schoolboys:*   *To become friends:*

Related expressions: Little by little

Step by step

3.57 Public outcry over

Meaning: People are very angry about something; there is a lot of media attention

Meaning in your language:

Usage: There is a public outcry over *A* (some topic)

1. There was a public outcry over the shoddy work methods used in construction of the nuclear power plant.

Shoddy work methods: *Nuclear power plant:*

2. The public outcry over the beef infected with mad cow disease caused some politicians to lose their jobs.

Infected: *Mad cow disease:*

3. The new security at the airports is the result of the public outcry over the bomb threats.

Airport security: *Bomb threats:*

Related expressions: A stink about

                             Raising Cain

3.58 Quoted as saying

Meaning: Somebody said something to a reporter.

Meaning in your language:

Usage: *A* (person) is quoted as saying *B* (reported speech)

1. The rock star was quoted as saying that his marriage next week would be held in a church.

Wedding held in a church:

2. An unidentified source in the mayor's office was quoted as saying that a new train station will be built next year.

Unidentified source: *Mayor's office:*

Train station:

3. The burglar was quoted as saying that he was badly mistreated in jail.

Burglar: *Mistreatment:*   *Jail:*

Related expressions: According to sources

                             On the record

3.59 Rapped (for)

Meaning: Someone is punished or criticized.

Meaning in your language:

Usage: **A** (person) is rapped for **B** (action)
1. The busboy was <u>rapped for</u> stealing money from the till.
Busboy: *The till:*
2. The teacher was <u>rapped</u> by the principal <u>for</u> not finishing the class on time.
Principal: *Not finishing on time:*
3. The plant manager was <u>rapped for</u> his lack of leadership during the emergency.
Plant manager: *Lack of leadership:*
Emergency:

Related expressions: In the hot seat

Take the heat

3.60 Rigged

Meaning: Someone cheated on a contest etc.

Meaning in your language:

Usage: **A** (race, contest, vote) is rigged by **B** (person, group)
1. The losing candidate believes that the election was <u>rigged</u> by the powerful ruling party.
Losing candidate: *Ruling party:*
2. The Russian beauty queen says the contest was <u>rigged</u> so that Miss America would win.
Beauty queen:
3. "In my opinion, the race was <u>rigged</u>. I didn't have a chance," the speed skater said.
Didn't have a chance: *Speed Skater:*

Related expression: A scam

A sting

3.61 Saber-rattling

Meaning: Someone makes threatening speeches, or tries to sound important or powerful.

Meaning in your language:

Usage: The *A* (action, speech) is saber-rattling
1. The government said that the provocative speech by the deposed dictator was just <u>saber-rattling</u>.
Deposed: *Dictator:*
2. The <u>saber-rattling</u> by the small Asian nation has political analysts worried about the threat of war.
Political analysts: *Threat of war:*
3. As soon as the country decided that it needed economic aid from the United Nations, the <u>saber-rattling</u> stopped.
Economic aid: *United Nations:*

Related expressions: Talking big

Hot air

3.62 Seen as a sign / warning

Meaning: The speaker is guessing about the meaning of something.

Meaning in your language:

Usage: *A* (action, event) is seen as *B* (meaning)
1. The recent increase the red tide in the river is <u>seen</u> by many scientists <u>as a sign</u> of water pollution.
Red Tide: *Water pollution:*
2. The influx of cheap labor is <u>seen as a warning</u> that immigration laws need to change.
Influx of: *Cheap labor:*
Immigration laws:
3. The poor test results are <u>seen as a sign</u> of problems with the educational system.
Poor test results: *Educational system:*

Related expressions: A taste of things to come

To take something as

3.63 Set to

Meaning: Something is ready to start, or will probably happen soon.

Meaning in your language:

Usage: **A** (person, object) is set to **B** (action) by/on **C** (time)

1. The space shuttle is <u>set to</u> take off at 8 PM EST.

Space shuttle: *Take off:*

EST (Eastern Standard Time):

2. The union representative is <u>set to</u> meet with the corporate rep this afternoon.

Union representative:

Corporate rep(resentative):

3. He's in great shape and is <u>set to</u> break a new world record at the next Olympics.

In great shape: *Break a record:*

Related expressions: To pencil someone in

                                       Nothing to do but wait

She is set to leave the hospital this afternoon

3.64 Good / poor showing

Meaning: The results (good or bad) of a test, election, etc.

Meaning in your language:

Usage: The good/poor showing of **A** (person, product)

1. The boxer's <u>poor showing</u> in the last three contests means that he will not be participating in the games in Melbourne next week.

Boxer: *To participate in the games:*

2. Because of his <u>good showing</u> in the municipal election, he is thinking of running for state governor next time.

Municipal election: *State governor:*

3. The <u>good showing</u> by the horse in the first race did not continue.

Related expressions: Pass with flying colors

The way things shaped up

3.65 Some / no leeway

Meaning #1: A compromise is possible/not possible.

Meaning in your language:

Usage: There is some/no leeway regarding **A** (situation)

1. Because of his contract, there was <u>no leeway</u> for the hockey player to retire.

Hockey player: *To retire:*

2. The new highway construction is scheduled to begin in the summer, but there is <u>some leeway</u> regarding the exact starting date.

Highway construction: *Starting date:*

Meaning #2: To be given freedom

Meaning in your language:

1. The judge granted the police <u>leeway to</u> record the woman's telephone conversations.

Judge: *To grant:*

To record phone conversations:

2. The professor granted him <u>leeway to</u> turn in his thesis after the deadline had passed.

To turn in a thesis: *Deadline:*

Related expressions: Room for negotiation (Meaning #1)

Carte blanche (Meaning #2)

3.66 Sooner or later

Meaning: Something is certain to happen, but nobody knows when.

Meaning in your language:

Usage: Sooner or later, *A* (action)

1. There will be a war <u>sooner or later</u> unless the two countries can learn to cooperate.

To learn to cooperate:

2. The company president can't hide forever. <u>Sooner or later</u> he is going to have to talk to the reporters.

Can't hide forever:

3. The doctor said that if the funding continues, a cure for cancer will be found <u>sooner or later.</u>

Funding: *Cure for cancer:*

Related expressions: One of these days

In the long run

3.67 Strong-arm tactics

Meaning: Using force to get something

Meaning in your language:

Usage: Strong-arm tactics by *A* (person, group)

1. The union leader said that they were very angry with the use of <u>strong-arm tactics</u> by the plant management.

Union leader: *Plant management:*

2. <u>Strong-arm tactics</u> may be necessary to remove the radicals who are blocking the entrance to the economic conference.

Radicals: *To block the entrance:*

Economic conference:

3. <u>Strong-arm tactics</u> are rarely as effective as fair play in negotiations.

Fair play: *Negotiations:*

Related expressions: Throwing your weight around

Heavy-handed

3.68 Subject to...

Meaning #1: A problem with something occurs occasionally.

Meaning in your language:

Usage: *A* (person, thing) is subject to *B* (problem, condition)
1. Because he has epilepsy, he is <u>subject to</u> seizures unexpectedly.
Epilepsy: *Seizures:*   *Unexpectedly:*
2. She has been <u>subject to</u> long periods of depression since she lost her job.
Long period: *Depression:*   *To lose a job:*
Meaning #2: [formal English] Part of a contract may change because of the situation.
Meaning in your language:
1. The contents of this menu are <u>subject to</u> change without notice.
Without notice:
2. Prices in this catalog are for the 2002 model of vehicle only, and are <u>subject to</u> change without notice.
The 2002 model of vehicle:

Related expressions: Prone to something (Meaning #1)

                             (Not) set in stone (Meaning #2)

He is subject to headaches

3.69 Sure to

Meaning: Something is probable or very likely to happen.

Meaning in your language:

Usage: **A** (fact, situation) is sure to **B** (action)
1. The new French restaurant is <u>sure to</u> be a smash when it opens next Wednesday.
French restaurant: *A smash:*
2. The speech by the Minister of State is <u>sure to</u> include a reference to women's rights.
Minister of State: *A reference to something:*
Women's rights:
3. The weather forecaster said that the temperature was <u>sure to</u> hit 40°C yesterday, but he was wrong.
Weather forecaster: *To hit … °C*

Related expressions: In the bag
                             Without fail

3.70 Tempered by

Meaning: Good news is balanced by bad news.

Meaning in your language:

Usage: **A** (fact, situation) is tempered by **B** (fact, situation)
1. His excitement about the job offer was <u>tempered by</u> his realization of how low the salary was.
Job offer: *Realization:*   *Low salary:*
2. Her love of money is <u>tempered by</u> her generous nature.
Love of money: *Generous nature:*
3. The perks of the singer's lavish lifestyle were <u>tempered by</u> her tiring promotional tour.
Perks: *Lavish lifestyle:*
Promotional tour:

Related expressions: Balanced by
                             Offset by

3.71 The ins and outs

Meaning: The details about something

Meaning in your language:

Usage: The ins and outs of **A** (topic)

1. I've never understood <u>the ins and outs</u> of bookkeeping.

Bookkeeping:

2. In Washington, you cannot advance socially if you don't know <u>the ins and outs</u> of politics.

To advance socially:

3. The company complained that the activists didn't understand <u>the ins and outs</u> of nuclear power.

To complain: *Activists:*

Nuclear power:

Related expressions: The nuts and bolts of

To know something inside out

3.72 The plight of the

Meaning: Some person or group is in a difficult or dangerous situation.

Meaning in your language:

Usage: The plight of the **A** (person, group) is **B** (opinion).

1. <u>The plight of the</u> physically challenged in this city is really sad.

Physically challenged (people):

2. <u>The plight of the</u> wild creatures living near the mining camp is upsetting many animal rights activists.

Wild creatures: *Upsetting:*

Animal rights activists:

3. The UN agency is studying <u>the plight of the</u> refugees during their difficult journey to a new country.

UN agency: *Refugees:*

Related expressions: A sorry state of affairs

A sob story

3.73 The stage is set for

Meaning: Everything is prepared or ready for something.

Meaning in your language:

Usage: The stage is set for *A* (event)

1. At the White House, <u>the stage is set for</u> the arrival of the heads of state this evening.

White House: *Heads of state:*

2. This economic downturn means that <u>the stage is set for</u> a number of new bankruptcies over the next few months.

Economic downturn: *Bankruptcies:*

3. The border skirmishes have <u>set the stage for</u> an increase in the number of asylum seekers.

Border skirmish: *Asylum seeker:*

Related expressions: Roll out the red carpet

Dog and pony show

3.74 (Only) the tip of the iceberg

Meaning: Something is only an example of a much larger situation.

Meaning in your language:

Usage: *A* (object, action, situation) is only the tip of the iceberg

1. The investigative authorities say that recent bribery allegations were <u>only the tip of the iceberg</u>.

Investigative authorities: *Bribery allegations:*

2. The spokesperson for the Ministry of Health and Welfare says that the recent case of food poisoning was <u>only the tip of the iceberg</u>. Many more cases are expected.

Spokesperson:

Ministry of Health and Welfare: *Food poisoning:*

3. The weather forecaster said that last week's hot weather was <u>the tip of the iceberg</u>.

Weather forecaster:

Related expressions: Taste of things to come

Opening gambit

3.75 The trail is hot / cold

Meaning #1: A search (often criminal investigation) is going well/badly.

Meaning in your language:

Usage: The trail is hot/cold for **A** (object, person)

1. The police say the trail <u>has gone cold</u> for the killer of the elderly local resident.

Killer: *Local resident:*

2. <u>The trail is hot</u> in the bank robbery case because there were many witnesses to the crime.

Bank robbery case: *Witnesses:*

Meaning #2: Someone is actively searching for something.

Meaning in your language:

1. The medical researchers <u>are hot on the trail</u> of a cure for the disease.

Medical researchers: *Cure for the disease:*

2. The reporters <u>were hot on the trail</u> of the heiress but she eluded them in the crowd.

Heiress: *To elude:*   *In the crowd:*

Related expressions: Plenty of leads/no leads (Meaning #1)

                                   In hot pursuit (Meaning #2)

3.76 Welcomed by

Meaning: Something is good news, or something is popular.

Meaning in your language:

Usage: **A** (action) is welcomed by **B** (person, group)

1. The new anti-noise bylaw <u>is welcomed by</u> people living in this small residential area.

Anti-noise bylaw: *Residential area:*

2. The reduction in the price of gasoline <u>is welcomed by</u> car owners.

Reduction:

3. The rainy weather <u>was welcomed by</u> farmers suffering from this year's drought.

Rainy weather: *To suffer from:*   *Drought(see 2.81):*

Related expressions: Music to one's ears

                                   A sigh of relief

3.77 With baited breath

Meaning: Someone is worried, or anxious to hear some news.

Meaning in your language:

Usage: *A* (person, group) waits with baited breath for *B* (news)

1. The boy's legal guardian waited <u>with baited breath</u> to hear any news about the arrest.

Legal guardian: *The arrest:*

2. The pregnant woman awaited the results of the blood test <u>with baited breath</u>.

Pregnant woman: *Blood test:*

3. The jockeys waited <u>with baited breath</u> to learn the results of the photo finish.

Jockey: *Photo finish:*

Related expressions: On pins and needles

Holding my breath

3.78 (A) Whitewash

Meaning: Someone lies, makes excuses, or hides something from the public.

Meaning in your language:

Usage: *A* (person, organization) whitewashes *B* (fact)

A (report) is a whitewash

1. The IOC member <u>whitewashed</u> the kickback by saying it was a loan.

IOC(International Olympic Committee):   *Loan:*

2. Even though he is a national hero, we shouldn't <u>whitewash</u> his faults.

National hero: *Faults:*

3. The widow called the official inquiry's report on her husband's fatal accident <u>a</u> total <u>whitewash</u>.

Widow: *Official inquiry:*   *Fatal accident:*

Related expressions: To brush aside (see 2.6)

A cover-up

Mini-Quiz: Expressions Part II

Part A

1. The architect's optimism about the design for the new building was … his understanding of how difficult it would be to construct.
a) welcomed by   **b)** rapped for   **c)** tempered by   **d)** some leeway

2. There is … in the negotiations and I think both sides will eventually reach an agreement.
a) off base   **b)** no stranger to   **c)** mud-slinging   **d)** some leeway

3. Crime is … and the police should be increasing their efforts.
a) saber-rattling   **b)** on the rise   **c)** on cloud nine **d)** off to a shaky start

4. The large financial donation by the radio station was … the volunteer group.
a) welcomed by   **b)** not worth   **c)** set to   **d)** off base

5. He is … controversy because of his unusual views on abortion and women's rights.
a) on the loose   **b)** quoted as saying   **c)** rapped for   **d)** no stranger to

6. It's … your arm is sore! You played golf all day yesterday.
a) no wonder   **b)** rapped for   **c)** subject to   **d)** off base

7. She has been … since her wedding engagement.
a) rigged   **b)** over time   **c)** on cloud nine   **d)** beyond me

8.These prices are … change without notice.

a) off the cuff   **b)** not worth   **c)** welcomed by   **d)** subject to

9.... refugees in Ethiopia is really very sad.

a) The ins and outs of   **b)** The stage is set for   **c)** Public outcry over   **d)** The plight of

10.... person in very good shape should try climbing Mt. Fuji.

a) Only a   **b)** No wonder   **c)** Off base   **d)** Saber-rattling

11. The use of cheap, portable CRT and MRI machines is …

a) set to   **b)** no comment   **c)** just around the corner   **d)** on the loose

12. Avoid … even if you are angry with your spouse.

a) mud slinging   **b)** over time   **c)** a good showing   **d)** sooner or later

13. Computers are only the …. Here at Electronics World!!!

a) rapped for   **b)** some leeway   **c)** off the cuff   **d)** tip of the iceberg

14. The manager's … remarks hurt the public image of the team.

a) over time   **b)** on the loose   **c)** public outcry   **d)** off the cuff

15. The snowfall is expected to decrease …

a) sure to   **b)** on the hot seat   **c)** on a limited basis   **d)** over time

Part B

1. The ins	a. of the iceberg
2. Mud	b. is hot
3. Public	c. limited basis
4. Just around	d. or later
5. Sooner	e. slinging
6. Quoted	f. rattling
7. Out of	g. is set for
8. Only the tip	h. the corner
9. Strong	i. as saying
10. With baited	j. the question
11. The stage	k. the cuff
12. Off	l. outcry
13. On a	m. breath
14. The trail	n. arm tactics
15. Saber	o. and outs

Part C

E.g. may / that / as / be / it : <u>Be that as it may</u>

1. around / just / corner / the : _____
2. basis / limited / on / a : _____
3. the / in / seat / hot : _____
4. out / question / of / the : _____
5. seen / of / sign / as / a : _____
6. ins / outs / the / and : _____
7. plight / the / the / of : _____
8. set / stage / for / is / the : _____
9. tip / the / the / of / iceberg : _____
10. trail / hot / is / the : _____

Final Test

Part A

1. How you could let your daughter marry such a terrible man…
a) is clamping down on   **b)** the trail is cold   **c)** is beyond me   **d)** with baited breath

2. The new cigarette tax … at midnight, so hurry up and buy some now!
a) goes into effect   **b)** give a green light to   **c)** on the loose   **d)** is subject to

3. The president … questions about his health, even though he looked quite ill.
a) brushed aside   **b)** fell through   **c)** got burned   **d)** no comment

4. Your son's night in jail will hopefully … never to lie to the police again.
a) brace for   **b)** duped into   **c)** teach him   **d)** sink in

5. The Ministry of Health is … the threat of a national epidemic.
a) crosshairs   **b)** taking seriously   **c)** fast approaching **d)** mud-slinging

6. There are … the resignation of the foreign minister because of his poor English.
a) take aim at   **b)** take a breather   **c)** sinking in   **d)** calls for

203

7.The annual Steinway piano competition always draws the…

a) public outcry   **b)** stave off   **c)** over time   **d)** cream of the crop

8.… efforts by local community members have resulted in the construction of a new library.

a) Crack-down   **b)** Fenced-in   **c)** On the bandwagon   **d)** Grassroots

9.The loss in the first match is definitely… the young player.

a) a setback to   **b)** pull out of   **c)** grassroots   **d)** opposed to

10. The American team has … the competition to protest the unfair decision by the umpire.

a) gained momentum   **b)** pulled out of   **c)** called for   **d)** welcomed by

11. The movie star is … that piece of real estate for her new beach resort.

a) is pressing charges   **b)** eyeing   **c)** a hit with   **d)** welcomed by

12. He had to … the burden of raising his three younger sisters after their parents were killed.

a) to step in   **b)** brace for   **c)** shoulder   **d)** fast approaching

13. …, you should lose some weight, give up smoking, and start exercising.

a) If you ask me   **b)** No matter how long   **c)** From left and right
d) Blowing the whistle on

14. Drive carefully today. The roads are quite slippery… the rain.

a) in the event of   **b)** tempered by   **c)** on account of   **d)** in full swing

15. Whether or not the food supplies reach the refugees in time to help them …

a) remains to be seen   **b)** strong-arm tactics   **c)** on the rise   **d)** in the cards

16. Many people have been … spending money on unnecessary medication.

a) over time   **b)** traded barbs   **c)** brushed aside   **d)** duped into

17. The mayor was… that anyone can be a success if they only work hard.

a) caused a stir   **b)** on the loose   **c)** off the cuff   **d)** quoted as saying

18. The movie … and the studio will probably lose millions of dollars.
a) falls on deaf ears   **b)** takes the stance   **c)** is a flop   **d)** shows promise

19. There was a lot of … in that debate instead of rational argument.
a) mud-slinging   **b)** war of words   **c)** fencing in   **d)** dogging

20. The country is small, but its communist government does a lot of …
a) pressing charges   **b)** saber-rattling   **c)** grassroots   **d)** falling on deaf ears

21. The government's decision to close the free medical clinic for the homeless has really…
a) spurred into action   **b)** ruffled some feathers   **c)** staved off   **d)** anyone's guess

22. You will have some good luck this week. …, you shouldn't gamble.
a) Thanks to   **b)** In spite of   **c)** In response to   **d)** Even so

23. … marriage, the hottest young star in Hollywood is now engaged.
a) Over time   **b)** Speaking of   **c)** Off the cuff   **d)** as a

24. … complaining all the time, maybe it's time to look for a new job.
a) If worse comes to worse   **b)** Instead of   **c)** In a move to   **d)** A bitter pill to swallow

25. The storm will certainly … over our weekend holiday plans.
a) cast a pall   **b)** a public outcry   **c)** be that as it may   **d)** from left and right

Part B

1. As far as...	a. breath
2. In the	b. of the
3. Considering	c. but to
4. To have no alternative	d. aside
5. To lie	e. benefit of the doubt
6. To clean	f. way to
7. To press	g. that
8. To tighten	h. ahead
9. To pour	i. as saying
10. To mark a	j. a lot of money into
11. To go into	k. effect
12. To follow in	l. up one's act
13. To brush	m. solid
14. To treat	n. the footsteps of
15. To walk on	o. light at the end of the tunnel
16. To see the	p. best of
17. To blow	q. charges
18. Quoted	r. new chapter in
19. Booked	s. wake of
20. With baited	t. seriously
21. The plight	u. eggshells
22. On the	v. one's belt
23. To give someone the	w. the whistle on
24. To make the	x. is concerned
25. To give	y. loose

Part C

E.g. may / that / as / be / it : <u>Be that as it may</u>

1. fuel / fire / to / to / add / the : _____
2. to / the / on / blow / whistle : _____
3. to / burn / oil / the / midnight : _____
4. in / niche / a / out / carve / to : _____
5. a / on / pall / cast / to : _____
6. to / stir / a / cause : _____
7. to / down / clamp / on : _____
8. up / one's / act / to / clean : _____
9. down / crack / to / on : _____
10. to / to / attention / draw : _____
11. worse / worst / to / if / comes : _____
12. event / in / of / the : _____
13. in / of / the / wake : _____
14. basis / on / a / limited : _____
15. on / other / the / hand : _____
16. is / to / say / that : _____
17. certain / a / to / extent : _____
18. pill / bitter / a / to / swallow : _____
19. fancy / flight / of / a : _____
20. a / the / of / minds / meeting : _____
21. up / an / and / comer : _____
22. chance / a / slim / of : _____
23. no / much / matter / how : _____
24. to / a / on / window / open : _____
25. seen / of / sign / as / a : _____
26. ins / outs / the / and : _____
27. plight / the / the / of : _____
28. set / stage / for / is / the : _____
29. tip / the / the / of / iceberg : _____
30. trail / hot / is / the : _____

207

Answers

Connectors:

Part A

1. b; 2. d; 3. c; 4. a; 5. d; 6. a; 7. c; 8. d; 9. b; 10. a; 11. b; 12. d; 13. a; 14. b; 15. c

Part B

1–e; 2–n; 3–b; 4–j; 5–a; 6–l; 7–i; 8–k; 9–d; 10–c; 11–m; 12–f; 13–h; 14–o; 15–g

Part C

1. If worst comes to worse; 2. In the event of; 3. In the wake of; 4. No matter how much; 5. On the other hand; 6. That is to say; 7. To a certain extent; 8. To be on the safe side; 9. To make a long story short; 10. As far as …. is concerned

Tips I

Crossword

Across: 2. page; 4. laptop; 5. online; 6. files; 10. internet; 11. engine; 12. cathode; 13. net
Down: 1. network; 2. processing; 3. link; 7. screen; 8. web; 9. slot

Verbs: Part I

Part A

1. b; 2. b; 3. a; 4. b; 5. a; 6. a; 7. d; 8. d; 9. d; 10. a; 11. b; 12. d; 13. a; 14. c; 15. a

Part B

1–o; 2–a; 3–f; 4–e; 5–n; 6–k; 7–d; 8–m; 9–i; 10–g; 11–c; 12–h; 13–l; 14–b; 15–j

Part C

1. To add fuel to the fire; 2. To blow the whistle on; 3. To burn the midnight oil; 4. To carve out a niche in; 5. To cast a pall on; 6. To cause a stir; 7. To clamp down on; 8. To clean up one's act; 9. To crack down on; 10. To draw attention to

Tips IV

Crossword

Across: 1. interest; 3. agency; 5. chronological; 6. grammar; 7. quotations; 9. background
Down: 1. important; 2. headline; 4. colorful; 5. current; 8. outcome

Verbs: Part II

Part A

1. d; 2. d; 3. c; 4. c; 5. a; 6. a; 7. c; 8. d; 9. b; 10. a; 11. a; 12. c; 13. d; 14. c; 15. b

Part B

1-m; 2-i; 3-a; 4-n; 5-b; 6-j; 7-k; 8-c; 9-h; 10-e; 11-o; 12-f; 13-g; 14-l; 15-d

Part C

1. To make a comeback; 2. To make the best of; 3. To mark a new chapter in; 4. To mark the first time that; 5. To open a window on; 6. To open its doors to; 7. To pour a lot of money into; 8. To pull out of; 9. To put on the market; 10. To remain to be seen

Tips VI

Crossword

Across: 3. exchange; 4. Price; 7. Earnings; 9. invest; 10. down; 11. state
Down: 1. interest; 2. Investment; 5. breakout; 6. conclusion; 8. lead

Expressions: Part I

Part A

1. b; 2. d; 3. d; 4. a; 5. d; 6. b; 7. a; 8. c; 9. d; 10. a; 11. b; 12. a; 13. c; 14. d; 15. b

Part B

1-f; 2-m; 3-i; 4-a; 5-c; 6-e; 7-b; 8-l; 9-k; 10-j; 11-n; 12-o; 13-g; 14-h; 15-d

Part C

1. A bitter pill to swallow; 2. A flight of fancy; 3. A meeting of the minds; 4. An up and comer; 5. A slim chance of; 6. A war of words; 7. A whole different ballgame; 8. Cream of the crop; 9. If you ask me; 10. In the cards

Tips VIII

Crossword

Across: 3. plate; 6. National; 7. core; 9. Hockey; 10. Baseball
Down: 1. Olympic; 2. steal; 3. Professional; 4. features; 5. Boxing; 8. body

Expressions: Part II

Part A

1. c; 2. d; 3. b; 4. a; 5. d; 6. a; 7. c; 8. d; 9. d; 10. a; 11. c; 12. a; 13. d; 14. d; 15. d

Part B

1-o; 2-e; 3-l; 4-h; 5-d; 6-i; 7-j; 8-a; 9-n; 10-m; 11-g; 12-k; 13-c; 14-b; 15-f

Part C

1. Just around the corner; 2. On a limited basis; 3. In the hot seat; 4. Out of the question; 5. Seen as a sign of; 6. The ins and outs; 7. The plight of the; 8. The stage is set for; 9. The tip of the iceberg; 10. The trail is hot

Final Test

Part A

1.c; 2. a; 3. a; 4. c; 5. b; 6. d; 7. d; 8. d; 9. a; 10. b; 11. b; 12. c; 13. a; 14. c; 15. a; 16. d; 17. d; 18. c; 19. a; 20. b; 21. b; 22. d; 23. b; 24. b; 25. a

Part B

1-x; 2-s; 3-g; 4-c; 5-h; 6-l; 7-q; 8-v; 9-j; 10-r; 11-k; 12-n; 13-d; 14-t; 15-u; 16-o; 17-w; 18-i; 19-m; 20-a; 21-b; 22-y; 23-e; 24-p; 25-f

Part C

1. To add fuel to the fire; 2. To blow the whistle on; 3. To burn the midnight oil; 4. To carve of a niche in; 5. To cast a pall on; 6. To cause a stir; 7. To clamp down on; 8. To clean up one's act; 9. To crack down on; 10. To draw attention to; 11. If worse comes to worst; 12. In the event of; 13. In the wake of; 14. On a limited basis; 15. On the other hand; 16. That is to say; 17. To a certain extent; 18. A bitter pill to swallow; 19. A flight of fancy; 20. A meeting of the minds; 21. An up and comer; 22. A slim chance of; 23. No matter how much; 24. To open a window on; 25. Seen as a sign of; 26. The ins and outs; 27. The plight of the; 28. The stage is set for; 29. The tip of the iceberg; 30. The trail is hot

David Petersen graduated from the University of Calgary with a B.Sc. in psychology. After acquiring a TESL certificate, he spent nearly 10 years teaching English in Japan, Hungary, and South Korea. He obtained a Ph.D. from the University of Malta in 2003, and then returned to Japan to earn a Level I on the National Japanese Proficiency Test. He currently lives in New Zealand where he works as a writer and freelance translator.

Other Books by David Petersen

www.lulu.com/lang-arts

Survivors: The A-bombed Trees of Hiroshima

Reading English News on the Internet: A Guide to Connectors, Verbs, Expressions, and Vocabulary for the **Japanese** ESL Student

An Invitation to Kagura: Hidden Gem of the Traditional Japanese Performing Arts

The Well-Tempered Body: Expressive Movement for Actors, Improvisers, and Performance Artists

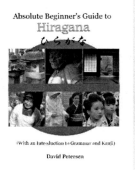

Absolute Beginner's Guide to Hiragana (With an Introduction to Grammar and Kanji)

09/2082/14
Z17.38

LaVergne, TN USA
10 March 2010
175560LV00001B/65/P